T0201144

Text as Data

Wiley and SAS Business Series

The Wiley and SAS Business Series presents books that help senior level managers with their critical management decisions.

Titles in the Wiley and SAS Business Series include:

The Analytic Hospitality Executive: Implementing Data Analytics in Hotels and Casinos by Kelly A. McGuire

Analytics: The Agile Way by Phil Simon

The Analytics Lifecycle Toolkit: A Practical Guide for an Effective Analytics Capability by Gregory S. Nelson

Anti-Money Laundering Transaction Monitoring Systems Implementation: Finding Anomalies by Derek Chau and Maarten van Dijck Nemcsik

Artificial Intelligence for Marketing: Practical Applications by Jim Sterne

Business Analytics for Managers: Taking Business Intelligence Beyond Reporting (Second Edition) by Gert H. N. Laursen and Jesper Thorlund

Business Forecasting: The Emerging Role of Artificial Intelligence and Machine Learning by Michael Gilliland, Len Tashman, and Udo Sglavo

The Cloud-Based Demand-Driven Supply Chain by Vinit Sharma

Consumption-Based Forecasting and Planning: Predicting Changing Demand Patterns in the New Digital Economy by Charles W. Chase

Credit Risk Analytics: Measurement Techniques, Applications, and Examples in SAS by Bart Baesen, Daniel Roesch, and Harald Scheule

Demand-Driven Inventory Optimization and Replenishment: Creating a More Efficient Supply Chain (Second Edition) by Robert A. Davis

Economic Modeling in the Post Great Recession Era: Incomplete Data, Imperfect Markets by John Silvia, Azhar Iqbal, and Sarah Watt House

Enhance Oil & Gas Exploration with Data-Driven Geophysical and Petrophysical Models by Keith Holdaway and Duncan Irving

Fraud Analytics Using Descriptive, Predictive, and Social Network Techniques: A Guide to Data Science for Fraud Detection by Bart Baesens, Veronique Van Vlasselaer, and Wouter Verbeke

Intelligent Credit Scoring: Building and Implementing Better Credit Risk Scorecards (Second Edition) by Naeem Siddiqi

JMP Connections: The Art of Utilizing Connections in Your Data by John Wubbel

Leaders and Innovators: How Data-Driven Organizations Are Winning with Analytics by Tho H. Nguyen

On-Camera Coach: Tools and Techniques for Business Professionals in a Video-Driven World by Karin Reed

Next Generation Demand Management: People, Process, Analytics, and Technology by Charles W. Chase

A Practical Guide to Analytics for Governments: Using Big Data for Good by Marie Lowman

Profit from Your Forecasting Software: A Best Practice Guide for Sales Forecasters by Paul Goodwin

Project Finance for Business Development by John E. Triantis

Smart Cities, Smart Future: Showcasing Tomorrow by Mike Barlow and Cornelia Levy-Bencheton

Statistical Thinking: Improving Business Performance (Third Edition) by Roger W. Hoerl and Ronald D. Snee

Strategies in Biomedical Data Science: Driving Force for Innovation by Jay Etchings

Style and Statistics: The Art of Retail Analytics by Brittany Bullard

Text as Data: Computational Methods of Understanding Written Expression Using SAS by Barry deVille and Gurpreet Singh Bawa

Transforming Healthcare Analytics: The Quest for Healthy Intelligence by Michael N. Lewis and Tho H. Nguyen

Visual Six Sigma: Making Data Analysis Lean (Second Edition) by Ian Cox, Marie A. Gaudard, and Mia L. Stephens

Warranty Fraud Management: Reducing Fraud and Other Excess Costs in Warranty and Service Operations by Matti Kurvinen, Ilkka Töyrylä, and D. N. Prabhakar Murthy

For more information on any of the above titles, please visit www.wiley.com.

Text as Data

Computational Methods of Understanding Written Expression Using SAS

By

Barry deVille and

Gurpreet Singh Bawa

WILEY

Copyright © 2022 by John Wiley & Sons, Inc. All rights reserved.

Published by John Wiley & Sons, Inc., Hoboken, New Jersey.
Published simultaneously in Canada.

No part of this publication may be reproduced, stored in a retrieval system, or
transmitted in any form or by any means, electronic, mechanical, photocopying,
recording, scanning, or otherwise, except as permitted under Section 107 or 108 of
the 1976 United States Copyright Act, without either the prior written permission
of the Publisher, or authorization through payment of the appropriate per-copy fee to
the Copyright Clearance Center, Inc., 222 Rosewood Drive, Danvers, MA 01923, (978)
750-8400, fax (978) 750-4470, or on the web at www.copyright.com. Requests to the
Publisher for permission should be addressed to the Permissions Department, John
Wiley & Sons, Inc., 111 River Street, Hoboken, NJ 07030, (201) 748-6011, fax (201)
748-6008, or online at http://www.wiley.com/go/permission.

Limit of Liability/Disclaimer of Warranty: While the publisher and author have
used their best efforts in preparing this book, they make no representations or
warranties with respect to the accuracy or completeness of the contents of this book
and specifically disclaim any implied warranties of merchantability or fitness for a
particular purpose. No warranty may be created or extended by sales representatives
or written sales materials. The advice and strategies contained herein may not be
suitable for your situation. You should consult with a professional where appropriate.
Neither the publisher nor author shall be liable for any loss of profit or any other
commercial damages, including but not limited to special, incidental, consequential, or
other damages.

For general information on our other products and services or for technical support,
please contact our Customer Care Department within the United States at (800) 762-
2974, outside the United States at (317) 572-3993 or fax (317) 572-4002.

Wiley also publishes its books in a variety of electronic formats. Some content that
appears in print may not be available in electronic formats. For more information
about Wiley products, visit our website at www.wiley.com.

Library of Congress Cataloging-in-Publication Data is Available:

9781119487128 (hardback)
9781119487173 (ePDF)
9781119487159 (ePub)

Cover Design: Wiley

SKY10029210_081921

To all those who unconditionally love and support authors and their writing processes – especially our life partners, Maya McNeilly and Dilpreet Kaur, who go above and beyond.

Contents

Preface

This book provides an end-to-end description of the text analytics process with examples drawn from a range of case studies using various capabilities of SAS text analytics and the associated SAS computing environment. Qualitative and quantitative approaches within the SAS environment are covered across the entire text analytics life cycle from document capture, document characterization, document understanding, through operational deployments.

We cover procedure-based, engineering approaches to text analytics, as well as more discovery-based quantitative approaches. Since much of the text analytics process depends on the text capture and text preprocessing environment, these aspects of text analytics are covered as well.

Acknowledgments

This work was initiated and promoted by Julie Palmieri, serving as editor-in-chief of SAS Press. James Allen Cox has consistently offered advice and review throughout and gave a detailed review of early versions of the draft. Tom Sabo gave advice and review and made significant contributions to the chapter on Boolean rules. Our colleagues Saratendu Sethi, Terry Woodfield, and Sanford Gayle have provided decades of advice on text analytics in general. Elisha Benjamin of John Wiley & Sons was a great source of advice and assistance throughout the project. Wiley executive editor Sheck Cho is the consummate professional and both a rock and a beacon for us aspiring authors.

As authors, we acknowledge their invaluable advice, assistance, encouragement, and also humbly acknowledge that any remaining faults are ours alone.

About the Authors

Barry deVille is a practitioner, developer, and author in the fields of statistics, data science, and text analytics. During a decades-long career at SAS, he collaborated extensively with the text analytic R&D development team, deploying text mining solutions to a variety of global clients in various industrial, financial, health, and social media applications. This work resulted in the award of numerous US patents on decision tree induction algorithms and multidimensional text analytics. Prior to joining SAS, he worked with the National Research Council and other government and commercial entities in Canada in the development and commercialization of statistical and machine learning algorithms.

Gurpreet Singh Bawa has practiced internationally in the areas of statistics with an emphasis on artificial intelligence (AI) and machine learning (ML). He was awarded a PhD at Panjab University, Chandigarh, India, in the fields of AI and ML. He has authored numerous publications in national and international journals. His research in the areas of unstructured data analysis have led to numerous patent applications and awards (including one with co-author deVille on social community identification and automatic document classification). He also works in breakeven analysis and portfolio optimization. He is currently authoring a book on advanced mathematics.

Text as Data

Introduction

Text analytics are a collection of computer methods that use semantic and numerical processing to convert collections of text into identified components that carry meaning and function and can be manipulated quantitatively. Meaning assignment is a semantic process that leads to greater understanding of the text. Numerical manipulation leads to a range of data summarization approaches that typically reduce complexity, capture multiple relationships, and highlight tendencies. Text analytics incorporates semantic and numerical text processing in a synergistic process that leads to greater understanding of various collections of text.

In this treatment we also touch on speech applications so we can see how spoken words, like written words, can be transformed into representations that can be manipulated and summarized quantitatively.

Chapter 1 expands our definition of text analytics and provides some background on the development of written language and systems of writing that are used to capture and communicate meaning.

Chapter 2 provides an overview of the end-to-end process of text analytics. A generic template is described that can enhance our understanding of the various aspects of text analytics and that can also serve as an organizing framework for discussing text analytics. These processes are further described in Chapter 3.

Linguistic processing and associated forms of document characterization are discussed in Chapter 4. Linguistic processing is the front-end text analytics intake process to read and parse the incoming text stream to identify useful and interesting textual components such as parts of speech, phrases, expressions, and special terms.

Chapter 5 shows how numerical approaches to data, including the production of dimensional summaries and data reduction approaches, can be productively applied to creating meaningful textual summaries and dimensional products, like text topics, that help us understand the content of text collections.

In Chapter 6 we provide examples of how quantitative text products can be used for classification and prediction tasks. A real-world industrial use case is discussed.

Chapter 7 discusses the architecture within SAS that unifies linguistic and quantitative processing and so blends the strengths of these two approaches. We show how Boolean rules are constructed, how these are derived from quantitative operations, and how they serve a linguistic purpose.

Chapter 8 provides a case study in speech processing and shows how audio signals can be analyzed and manipulated much like text products to create analytical reports.

There is also a glossary of specialized terms and three appendices. Appendix A expands on the discussion of text characterization and provides an example of how mood state extracted from text can be used in text analytics. Appendix B provides a discussion and architectural approach to using audio processing to infer end user persona characteristics in the construction of artificial intelligence computer-user interaction interfaces. Appendix C provides an annotated summary description of critical patents that have been assigned to SAS. A range of important patents are covered, including an initial patent awarded to extract dimensional products from text and some of the more recent patents that address the unified approach to linguistic and numerical processing.

CHAPTER **1**

Text Mining and Text Analytics

This chapter describes some of the background and recent history of text analytics and provides real-world examples of how text analytics works and solves business problems. This treatment provides examples of common forms of text analytics and examples of solution approaches. The discussion ranges from a history of the analytical treatment of text expression up to the most recent developments and applications.

BACKGROUND AND TERMINOLOGY

The analysis of written and spoken expression has been developing as a computer application over several decades. Some of the earliest research in machine learning and artificial intelligence dealt with the problem of reading and interpreting text as well as in text translation (machine translation). These early activities gave rise to a field of computer science known as *natural language processing (NLP)*. The recent rapid development of computer power – including processing power, large data, high bandwidth communication, and cloud-based, high-capacity computer memory – has provided a major new (and considerably broadened) emphasis on computerized text processing and text analysis.

TEXT ANALYTICS: WHAT IS IT?

Text processing and text analysis are components of the developing area of understanding written and spoken expression. Commonly occurring text documents – such as traditional newspapers, journals and periodicals, and, more recently, electronic documents, such as social media posts and emails – are forms of written expression. This active, multilayered area in current computer applications joins well-established, traditional fields such as linguistics and literary analysis to form the outline of the emerging field we call *text analytics*.

Current approaches to text analytics operate in two reinforcing directions that incorporate traditional forms of linguistic and literary analysis with a wide range of statistical, artificial intelligence (AI), and cognitive computing techniques to effectively process written and spoken expressions. The decoded expressions are used to drive a wide range of computer-mediated inference tasks that includes artificial intelligence, cognitive computing, and statistical inference. An everyday example is when we speak or type in a destination in order to receive an optimal driving route. Similarly, a call center agent might decipher multiple forms of common requests in order to construct the most effective solution approach.

Our treatment throughout the chapters to come includes examples of common forms of text analytics and examples of solution approaches. The discussion ranges from a history of the analytical treatment of text expression up to the most recent developments and applications. Since speech is quickly becoming an important form of unstructured data, a final chapter takes up the topic of rendering speech to text.

Computer science and AI emerged as formal disciplines in the aftermath of World War II. An early application of computers to the analysis of written expression, natural language processing, took a universal approach, designed to apply regardless of what language the text was written in – English, Spanish, or Chinese. The techniques that have been developed also apply regardless of the source of the text to be analyzed. With the widespread availability of speech-to-text engines, it is also possible to consider a wide variety of spoken documents as potential sources for text analytics.

An important goal of NLP is to decompose text constructs (sentences, paragraphs, articles, chapters) into various kinds of entities, verbs, semantic constructs (like articles and conjunctions), and so on. The sentence "See Spot run" may be processed and encoded into an NLP representation as: declarative sentence (intransitive); Spot – Subject (Animal/Dog); run – Verb (motion).

Historically, NLP relied on various linguistic analysis capabilities, including extensive logical processing and reasoning capabilities. As computing capabilities have expanded, NLP has increasingly relied on a range of computational approaches to enhance the range of NLP results. An emerging area of NLP includes statistical natural language processing (SNLP). This form of NLP can be used to craft high-level representations of textual documents so that relationships between and among the documents can be computed statistically. The statistical capability also improves the accuracy of the NLP processing itself.

One recent area of written language processing includes statistical document analysis (SDA). Like SNLP, SDA enables us to show the statistical relationships between and among the various components of a textual document. Further, it enables us to summarize the document using multivariate statistical techniques like cluster analysis and latent class analysis. Predictive analytics such as regression analysis, decision trees, and neural networks can also be used.

As computer processing and storage have continued to grow, so too have a variety of deep learning applications. One such application is the Bidirectional Encoder Representations from Transformers (BERT), a deep-learning application for research at Google AI language.[i]

BERT can be leveraged for tasks such as categorization, entity extraction, and natural language generation. Deep learning approaches require significant computing power and training. As the area of text analytics continues to unfold, we will likely see how deep learning approaches complement the capabilities offered in traditional text analytics, which are less computationally intensive and more than adequate for a wide range of tasks.

The fields of *text mining* and *text analytics* are recent applied areas of SDA used in a variety of general-purpose social and economic settings. Text mining often refers to the construction of statistical or numerical models or predictions. Common sources of data include customer service logs and emails, customer use records for warranty issue analysis and defect detection. Text analytics often refers to semantically based applications – for example, customer analytics (who talks to whom and what do they say?), competitive analysis (brand metrics, mentions), and content management (the creation of taxonomies, web page characterization).

Brief History of Text

Language is a form of communication, and text is a written form of language. Text comes in a variety of symbolic forms. In addition to the alphabetic representation we see capturing the written expression in this text, there are other encoding systems such as syllabaries that capture spoken syllables and logograms that capture pictographic representations. Linguistics distinguishes between phonograms – which

Figure 1.1 Traffic sign in Cherokee syllabary, Tahlequah, Oklahoma.
Source: Shot November 11, 2007. By Uyvsdi. License: Public Domain.

capture parts of words like syllables in written expression – and logograms – which capture entire concepts.

Figure 1.1 shows an example of a pictographic representation – the STOP sign itself – an alphabetic representation (in Latin script) that spells the word "STOP" and a syllabary – in this case, one used to record the Cherokee language.

One of the earliest true writing systems, dating to the third millennium BCE, was cuneiform, originally a pictographic writing system that eventually evolved into a variety of alphabetic representations. One intermediate form of simplified cuneiform was Old Persian. It included a semi-alphabetic syllabary, using far fewer wedge strokes than earlier Assyrian versions of cuneiform. It included a handful of logograms for frequently occurring words such as "god" and "king" (see Figure 1.2).

Chinese characters evolved in the second millennium BCE and, according to sources such as Dong,[ii] were first organized into a comprehensive writing system during the Qin dynasty (259–210 BCE).

Figure 1.2 Example of cuneiform recording the distribution of beer in southern Iraq, 3100–3000 BCE.
Source: BabelStone, Licensed under CC BY-SA 3.0.

These characters eventually gave rise to the widespread use of the characteristic logograms of Chinese in Asia (see Figure 1.3).

The representation of different writing systems is important for mapping language meanings between languages. Figure 1.4 shows a modern representation of the Chinese character for eye and the associated Latin script representation to show the translation between a pictograph (logogram) and syllabary.

Figure 1.3 Shang oracle bone script for character "Eye." Modern character is 目.
Source: Tomchen1989. Public Domain.

Mù

Figure 1.4 Modern Chinese representation of "eye" (mù).
Source: B. deVille.

Writing Systems of the World

Writing systems of the world that have evolved from ancient times to the present day can be organized into five categories[iii]: alphabets, abjads, abugidas, syllabaries, and logo-syllabaries.

1. **Alphabets.** Each letter represents a sound which can be either a consonant or a vowel. English uses an alphabet as do such related languages as French, German, and Spanish.

2. **Abjads.** Similar to alphabets except they are made up primarily of consonants. Vowel markings are absent or partial and may or may not be present. Hebrew and Arabic are the two main abjads in use today.

3. **Abugidas.** These are writing systems where consonant-vowel sequences are written as a unit. Consonants form the main units in the system and may stand alone or carry vowel notations with them. Abugidas evolved from a pre-Common Era Indian script called Brahmi and are prevalent in Southeast Asia.

4. **Syllabaries.** Here each character represents an entire syllable. A syllable is normally one consonant and one vowel. Japanese is an example.

5. **Logo-syllabary.** Each character can stand for a unique symbol or an entire word or idea. Chinese is an example.

Meaning and Ambiguity

Much of the work that we do in text mining – both hidden in the various text analytics engines we use as well as in the explicit user interventions we employ – will be directed at getting the best, most unambiguous meaning from the words or terms we use in the analysis. Numbers have relatively unambiguous properties and this facilitates their use in analytics. When we use *test*, however, it is normal to have a certain level of ambiguity in meaning. One of the main reasons for this is that textual terms are polysemous – one term may have multiple meanings. As an example of polysemy, think about the question, "Did you get it?" The question could be asking about understanding ("Yes, I understood!"), fetching an object ("I picked up the ladder this morning"), or receiving goods or services ("I got the vaccine last Tuesday").

Spoken and written forms of communication are prone to other breakdowns in communication. Figure 1.5 provides a rough illustration of the key features that are part of communication. One the earliest approaches to capturing and quantifying the information loss or gain contained in communication was the concept of entropy, formulated by Claude Shannon.[iv] Shannon borrowed the concept from thermodynamics and used it to rigorously engineer the communications properties of a range of communications methods and devices while working for Bell Labs. His contributions have placed him in the ranks of major figures in the establishment of the "computer age" along with such figures as Von Neuman, Alan Turing, Robert Noyce, Norbert Weiner, and Geoffrey Moore. As shown in the example in Figure 1.5, this approach is still used today.

The send–receive communications model reflects the notion of communication as capturing some kind of representation of an object that has been identified and passing the representation through various processing stages until the object representation has been received and decoded. In each of the processing stages, there is an opportunity for representation error to creep in so the message can degrade.

We can all informally observe the operation of entropy as we play the parlor game of passing a message from ear-to-ear in a circle of people. Words perfectly communicate when all the elements of the

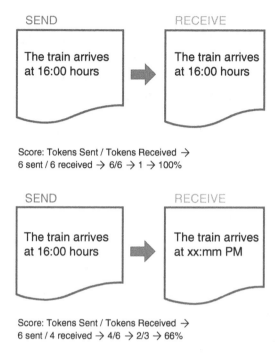

Score: Tokens Sent / Tokens Received →
6 sent / 6 received → 6/6 → 1 → 100%

Score: Tokens Sent / Tokens Received →
6 sent / 4 received → 4/6 → 2/3 → 66%

Figure 1.5 Encode–decode send–receive communications model.
Source: B. deVille.

sender's message are completely and accurately received and interpreted by the receiver.

Figure 1.5 provides an illustration of how entropy is calculated. When the full sentence (six tokens) is fully sent and received correctly there is 100 percent communication (zero entropy). When parts of the sentence are miscommunicated, for example, only four tokens are received; then communication drops to 66 percent. In this simple example, the first communication is better than the second communication (and there is an associated information gain of one-third, or over 33 percent).

Since text is a form of communication, we can gauge the accuracy and interpretation of the meaning of text using notions and measures of information entropy and information gain. Upon closer examination, we can also see that entropy and the statistical notion of correlation or association are related. The lower the entropy, the higher the correlation. As we move more deeply into text analytics, the precision of textual meaning – sometimes reflected by low entropy and high association measures – becomes important, especially when we use text analytics to analyze large volumes of data. As with all data analysis tasks, the greater the accuracy of the analysis, the more useful the insights.

As a simple example of how we might calculate entropy, let's say we have documents about trains and boats. For purpose of illustration, we will use a radically simplified example in Table 1.1.

The "train" documents have the following words or tokens:

train wheels diesel track land

The "boat" documents have the following words or tokens:

boat rudder sail sea water

At this point, we can reframe the collection of text documents into a classification scheme that provides us with the ability to explore the communicative properties of words in a structured, reproducible fashion.

Table 1.1 Trains and Boats Example: Document Collection

Document	Class	Component words/tokens							
		wheels	rudder	diesel	sail	track	sea	land	water
1	TRAIN	X		X		X	X	X	X
2	BOAT		X		X				
3	TRAIN	X		X		X		X	X
4	BOAT	X			X		X	X	
5	TRAIN	X							
6	BOAT		X			X	X		X
7	TRAIN	X						X	
8	BOAT		X			X	X		
9	TRAIN	X							
10	BOAT				X	X		X	
11	TRAIN	X	X			X		X	X
12	BOAT	X		X			X	X	X

We can see that some terms/tokens appear in both kinds of documents: trains and boats. We can use entropy calculations to tell us which terms have the least entropy and are therefore most useful in classifying a document.

Shannon's formula for entropy (information theory) is . . .

$$H(X) = -p\log_2(p) - q\log_2(q)$$

where H(X) is the expected value of the entropy calculation. It measures the difference in the probability of two outcomes, p and q.

In our example, p and q indicate whether the vehicle class is "train" or "boat." Logarithms have many useful properties, and the base 2 is used to support binary outcomes. This formula tells us that the expected entropy calculation of the features wheels through water in the above table will be formed by taking the logarithms of the probability of the features associated with one class – *train* – minus the probability of the features associated with the alternative class – *boat*.

If we calculate the entropy of the various terms in the example document (Table 1.2), we will see that the most useful term to unambiguously classify a document has the lowest entropy. This term is "sail." A high-entropy term like "diesel" is highly ambiguous, since it is applied to trains and boats with equal frequency.

Table 1.2 Entropy Calculation for Trains and Boats Example

Feature	Proportion (train)	Proportion (boat)	pr(train)	pr(boat)	Entropy
wheels	6/8	2/8	0.75	0.25	0.811
rudder	1/4	3/4	0.25	0.75	0.811
diesel	2/4	2/4	0.50	0.50	1
sail	0/3	3/3	0	1	0
track	3/5	2/5	0.60	0.40	0.971
sea	1/6	5/6	0.17	0.83	0.65
land	4/6	2/6	0.67	0.33	0.918
water	2/5	3/5	0.40	0.60	0.971

NOTES

i. J. Devlin, M. W. Chang, K. Lee, and K. Toutanova, *BERT: Pre-training of Deep Bidirectional Transformers for Language Understanding Google AI Language* (Ithaca, NY: Cornell University: 2019). https://arxiv.org/abs/1810.04805v2.

ii. H. T.O. Dong, *A History of the Chinese Language* (London and New York: Routledge, 2014).

iii. F. Coulmas, *The Writing Systems of the World* (Hoboken, NJ: Wiley-Blackwell, 1919).

iv. J. J. Soni and R. Goodman, *A Mind at Play: How Claude Shannon Invented the Information Age* (New York: Simon & Schuster, 2017).

CHAPTER 2

Text Analytics
Process Overview

TEXT ANALYTICS PROCESSING

In this chapter, we identify a number of best practices in the areas of machine learning, data and text mining, and analytics processing. A few processing templates have evolved for data mining and machine learning.[i] The cloud-enabled approach adopted by SAS is summarized in SAS Institute Inc.[ii] This is a fast-moving area where new practices evolve constantly.

PROCESS BUILDING BLOCKS

A high-level view of processing for text analytics resembles many solution approaches in information technology. This section looks at the primary building blocks often used in text analytics:

- **Preparation.** Getting the text ready for analysis (data capture, text decomposition, mapping to a data representation)
- **Utilization.** Interpretation and deployment.

Figure 2.1 describes the life cycle of text analytics from capture to deployment in six major processes. We can map document capture, test-to-data transfer, and characterization in the *preparation* phase.

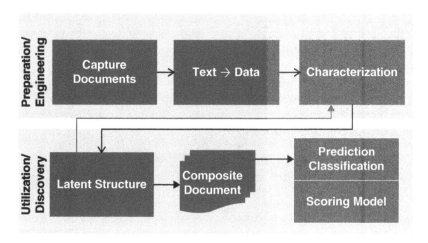

Figure 2.1 Main stages of the text-mining process.
Source: B. deVille.

We can map latent structure development, composite document assembly, and prediction/classification in the *utilization* phase.

Preparation

- **Capture documents.** First, assemble the documents. Usually, text documents require some kind of preprocessing to bring them into the analysis environment. For example, articles may be scraped from the web (or from blogs), document repositories may be exported, a range of formats such as .pdf, .txt, and .doc may need to be imported. The inclusion of written text symbols in standard alphabetic and often pictographic form presents an additional layer of complexity over and above the collection of metric or numerical data. Audio input, in the form of speech, can also be preprocessed to create phonetic data that can be converted into a number of text products.

- **Text-to-data.** Once the document is placed in text format, it may be parsed using a variety of techniques. Traditional methods include natural language processing (NLP). The most common form of NLP tags the terms in text fragments by a part of speech identifier such as noun, verb, adjective, adverb, and so on. NLP also tags the document with entities – so names, brands, addresses, quantities, and even specialized descriptors such as machine parts are identified. Other common steps include stemming, assigning synonyms, correcting spelling, and such macro-document processes as identifying topics, subtopics, and other parts of documents.

- **Characterization.** This step includes the procedural construction of text products based primarily on engineered NLP processes. It also includes, in a feedback fashion, the text products of dimensional reduction carried on in downstream processes. Mood or sentiment scores are often calculated in this step. When mood or sentiment scores are calculated for the document collection, then a high-level summary of mood or sentiment can also be produced. Dimensional products, such as clusters and topics, can also be inserted into the documents collection; this can facilitate global collection summarization by incorporating topics or clusters in corpus summaries. It is also possible to use various network representations to surface the linkages between terms and clusters. Cluster and topic products can also form the basis for the production of an abstract in standardized form (e.g., with all the entities identified, misspellings corrected, and the synonyms applied). Entities can be identified through built in named-entity recognition facilities or through rules-based approaches such as those provided by the SAS language interpretation for textual information (LITI).

Another rich set of operations in this area includes the identification of sequences of terms, words, or tokens taken in combination with one another. One promising area of research is reported by Cox and Allbright, which attempts to construct unambiguous combinations of terms that have greater meaning and predictive power than simple words or word-combinations taken in literal sequence (without contextual processing).[iii]

Utilization

■ **Latent structure/dimension reduction.** This step incorporates statistical algorithms to form high-level, compressed representations of the text as factor scores or clusters. This is typically a statistical approach that takes the parsed representation of the document in order to represent the meaning in a summarized form. This process is called *dimension reduction* because the numerical approaches take many objects and attributes and represent them into a smaller number of objects with a smaller number of shared attributes. A common example is a representation of the full continuous spectrum of light into red, yellow, green, blue categories. Typical dimensional reductions employed here are clusters, factorizations (which result in factor scores and latent attributes), and roll-up terms. Other possibilities include topics and term groupings, which combine multiple terms together as "*n*-grams."

- **Composite document.** The composite document contains the original text, the preprocessed text, and the results of the dimensional reduction. We can also provide for the introduction of other data sources and contextual information. Typical dimension reduction products include singular value decomposition (SVD) scores (which may be treated as latent semantic constructs or can be transformed into topics), rollup terms, and document-clustering products.

- **Prediction and classification.** This is used to employ text-mined results in the generation of a predictive score or classification. Customer intent may be estimated (likelihood to buy or defect), or document type may be assigned (warranty classification, defect type).

- **Scoring model.** Many scoring models are available and may be in functional form (e.g., equations) or rules form (if . . . then . . . else). The scoring models can be deployed in a variety of environments and are capable of processing and displaying the contents of new, previously unprocessed text documents.

PROCESS DESCRIPTION

Text Mining Data Sources

There are many kinds of text data repositories and many kinds of original textual data sources. For applied business and industrial applications, the data source may often be a host website or perhaps a social media data selection. The text mining and text analytics site at UC Berkeley provides an example of the many different data sources available: https://guides.lib.berkeley.edu/text-mining. Links to many different data sources are provided on this web location, including books (including over 50,000 volumes available on Project Gutenberg), newspapers and magazines, scholarly journals, government documents, linguistic corpora, literature, social media archives, and historical collections. Github also contains hundreds of text databases: https://github.com/awesomedata/awesome-public-datasets.

Capture

Regardless of the data source, a number of data on-boarding tasks are required to turn the raw textual data into useful sources of analytical insight:

- **Ensure code compatibility.** Increasingly, in an era of global formats it is important to ensure compatibility of all types of textual data – including logograms and even emoticons. Usually this means turning on the input encoding to a more robust format than standard American ASCII and to use a format such as UCS-8, for example.

- **Determine access method/structure.** There are many utilities, such as SAS's tmfilter, that provide transparent access to various data sources and websites. Some locations provide their own API (application programmer's interface), such as https://dev.elsevier.com/tecdoc_text_mining.html.

Another common method uses the computer's folder or directory structure to store text and examples. This is useful for training classification tasks where the structure is used as the target class and the text documents in the location are used as training instances. As shown in Figure 2.2, the top-level folder/directory name is *Category Folder Structure*. It contains three subfolders in this example: Business; Sports, and Music. In typical applications, documents most related to business would be in the Business folder; those relating

Figure 2.2 Category-oriented folder structure.
Source: B. deVille.

to sports would be in the Sports folder, and so on. Later, when the text-learning system needs to find linguistic rules that characterize and distinguish Business documents from Music documents, these folders and associated documents will be used as training data to learn the rules.

LINGUISTIC PROCESSING

Once we have stored and identified the text that we want to work, we are ready to rework the qualitative, textual data into quantitative data products that supports more robust computation. The general term for this stage of the text analytic process is *linguistic processing*.

Linguistic processing is the text analytic ability to perform detailed linguistic operations on a term-by-term basis as the linguistic processor moves through the document in line-by-line and term-by-term sequence. Although this is the first step in creating the term by document matrix that is the basis for the higher-dimension, numeric linear algebra approaches that are the hallmark of advanced text analytics, linguistic processing is a key enabler and also a significant approach in its own right.

Once the text has been assembled, it is viewed by the parse engine as a sequence of characters that are encoded in some text or image representation.

A process overview of text treatments, transformations, derivations, and extractions are listed in Figure 2.3 and briefly described as follows:

- **Tokenization.** Here we use punctuation and character encoding to identify document sections, words, terms, and images (where appropriate). Figure 2.4 provides an example of text that is used to illustrate tokenization in the context of document parsing.
- **Consolidation.** Spell checking is usually performed as part of this step. Here we stem words (look for the root word) and expand or lemmatize words (map terms to a common root). The main goal of stemming and lemmatization is to create a common representation of various forms of the same word.

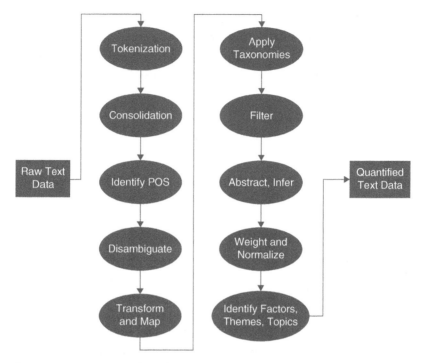

Figure 2.3 Text treatments, transformations, derivations, and extractions.
Source: B. deVille.

- ▥ **Identify parts of speech and named entities.** Isolate and identify parts of speech (POS) and associate with words and terms. Isolate special words and named entities (NE) like dates, proper names, locations, and noun phrases.
- ▥ **Disambiguate.** Word sense disambiguation is used to infer the semantic meaning of a word. The text segment "bank," for example, can have many meanings; e.g., it could be a financial institution, the physical building that houses a financial institution, a ridge on a pool table, or the edge of a river. Text terms are disambiguated based on the context as found in the source document, sometimes called a *semantic field*. For example, the phrase "you can bank on that" contains a verb that probably relates to financial institutions, while "he banked it off the left bunker" is more likely related to the game of pool.

- **Transform.** The most common transformation is *stemming* and *lemmatization*. Other transformations include correcting spelling errors, resolving upper and lower case variations as well as applying synonyms and acronyms.

- **Apply mappings.** Extract common term expansions for standard tables such as metropolitan area, geography (country, state, and so on), and business codes such as Standard Industrial Classification (SIC).

- **Apply taxonomy, typology, or ontology.** A wide range of taxonomies, typologies, ontologies, and classification systems may also be used in a more general application of the mapping and transformation process.

- **Filter.** Most frequently, this includes the use of start lists and stop lists to indicate which terms will "only" be used – i.e., a start list – and which words will be dropped or hidden – i.e., a stop list. Particular terms may also be hidden based on various criteria such as word frequency.

- **Abstract, infer.** Abstractions take word or token sequences and build them into special-purpose indicators. Common abstractions are *n*-grams, which are concatenated words or terms and are typically adjacent to one another in the text stream. Inferences are used to identify special text products – like mood, sentiment, or author inferences (e.g., gender).

- **N-grams.** In cases where the individual documents are lengthy and consist of lots of content, such as in the case of books, it makes sense to analyze at a paragraph or sentence level, since the latent idea most likely remains stable across sentences and paragraphs. However, in our example, we have short, terse feedback for products consumed by users; thus, a word or *n*-gram level tokenization is suitable to capture this finer level of detail.

N-grams are contiguous sequences of *n* objects from a piece of text. These objects can be anything – from words to phonemes, or any aggregated text element depending on the task requirement. Table 2.1 illustrates *n*-grams with words as objects.

Table 2.1 *N*-gram Illustration

Sentence: "A swimmer likes swimming, thus he swims."	
Unigram (1-gram)	A, Swimmer, likes, swimming, thus, he, swims, . . .
Bigram (2-gram)	A swimmer, swimmer likes, likes swimming, swimming thus, . . .
Trigram (3-gram)	A swimmer likes, swimmer likes swimming, likes swimming thus, . . .

Table 2.2 Advantage of Using *n*-grams vs. Unigrams

The packaging was not good.	Unigram	The, packaging, was, not, good.
	Bigram	The packaging, Packaging was, was not, not good.

The simple and easiest method of *n*-gram tokenization is to use unigrams. Here, individual words are considered as features that might explain some consumer behavior. Although this is an easy approach, one downside is that it is easy to lose the capability of differentiating "not good" and "not" and "good" separately. Table 2.2 shows a comparison of Unigrams and Bigrams and demonstrates the extra information that is encoded in the Bigram representation. Since *n*-grams consist of contiguous co-occurring words, they maintain a level of context in the original document text, such as the capability to distinguish between "white house" in a context of home paints or politics. *N*-grams are also useful for maintaining context, for example, maintaining "not" with "good."

- **Weight and normalize.** Upweight and downweight terms for emphasis; for example, to highlight rare terms or deemphasize frequent terms. Terms may also be standardized or normalized so, for example, their frequency in a document is converted to a normal score (*z*-score), high frequency or low frequency terms may be weight-adjusted; this impacts the computation of various text products such as clusters and topics.

- **Term frequency inverse document frequency (TFIDF).** One of the most useful weighting approaches is TFIDF because the frequency of a term is adjusted by dividing by the overall frequency of the term in the entire collection. This affects specificity so rare terms are upweighted while common terms that would otherwise swamp the analysis are downweighed. The TFIDF weight comprises of two parts:

1. **Normalized term frequency (TF).** Enumeration of how many times the token occurs within a document, divided by the token count of the document.

2. **Inverse document frequency (IDF).** The logarithmic transformation of the total count of documents in the corpus divided by the count of documents in which the specific token in question occurs.

To summarize:

$$\text{TF}(t) = (\# \text{ times token } t \text{ occurs in a document}) / (\# \text{ tokens in the document}).$$

$$TF_{ij} = \log(tf_{ij} + 1); tf_{ij} = n_{ij} / N_j$$

where n_{ij} represents the count of times i^{th} word is present in the jth document.

$$\text{IDF}(t) = \log e \ (\# \text{ documents} / \# \text{ documents containing token } t).$$

$$\text{IDF } i = \log |D| / n_i$$

Here $|D|$ is the total cardinality of documents in the corpus and n_i represents the count of documents in which the ith word is present.

Thus, the measure TFIDF(t) = TF(t) * IDF(t).

■ **Identify factors, themes, topics.** Many data summarization techniques are designed to compress multiple data dimensions into a lower number of dimensions to make the data more tractable and understandable. Many of these techniques are appropriate for text once the textual data has been parsed, transformed, and assigned to a data structure with associated meta data. These techniques are discussed later, primarily in Chapter 5.

Parsing and Parse Products

Let's begin our discussion of parsing by looking at a simple example. In our case, let's look at one of the most famous speeches of all time – in this case, the fictional eulogy given by Mark Antony at Julius Caesar's burial in the eponymous play by William Shakespeare.

In this case, the poetry foundation[iv] was accessed to provide the text displayed in Figure 2.4

- **Tokenization.** All the spaces in the document have been identified as "." and the end of line character is also displayed at the end of each line.

- **Spaces and end-of-line (EOL) characters**. These characters are used as delimiters in consuming the original text and building a table of parse products. The text analytics parse engine consumes the text in a way that uses grammar rules to identify the various parts of speech in the document. In this way, the first line of the oration is read as shown in Table 2.3.

- **Consolidation (stemming or lemmatization).** One strategy to simplify the consolidation of variations of a word-term is to strip off plural representations, like "Romans," and express these word-terms in singular form, like "roman." This step facilitates the process of grouping word-terms together according to meaning regardless of the grammatical spelling and particular form; for example, "am," "are," "is" forms of the verb "to be" becomes the simplified stem form of "be."

- **Disambiguation.** Notice that although the parser would use the capitalization of Friends and Romans as information to determine part of speech, the capitalization will normally be stripped off and all word-terms will be stored internally in lower case. The representation of all word-terms in lower case is one of the first steps that the parser takes in an effort to disambiguate the meaning of multiple terms. Therefore, *Romans* and

```
Friends, ·Romans, ·countrymen, ·lend ·me ·your ·ears; ⌐
I ·come ·to ·bury ·Caesar, ·not ·to ·praise ·him. ⌐
The ·evil ·that ·men ·do ·lives ·after ·them; ⌐
The ·good ·is ·oft ·interred ·with ·their ·bones; ⌐
So ·let ·it ·be ·with ·Caesar. ·The ·noble ·Brutus ⌐
Hath ·told ·you ·Caesar ·was ·ambitious: ⌐
If ·it ·were ·so, ·it ·was ·a ·grievous ·fault, ⌐
And ·grievously ·hath ·Caesar ·answer'd ·it. ⌐
Here, ·under ·leave ·of ·Brutus ·and ·the ·rest— ⌐
For ·Brutus ·is ·an ·honourable ·man; ⌐
So ·are ·they ·all, ·all ·honourable ·men— ⌐
Come ·I ·to ·speak ·in ·Caesar's ·funeral. ⌐
He ·was ·my ·friend, ·faithful ·and ·just ·to ·me: ⌐
But ·Brutus ·says ·he ·was ·ambitious; ⌐
And ·Brutus ·is ·an ·honourable ·man. ⌐
He ·hath ·brought ·many ·captives ·home ·to ·Rome ⌐
Whose ·ransoms ·did ·the ·general ·coffers ·fill: ⌐
Did ·this ·in ·Caesar ·seem ·ambitious? ⌐
When ·that ·the ·poor ·have ·cried, ·Caesar ·hath ·wept: ⌐
Ambition ·should ·be ·made ·of ·sterner ·stuff: ⌐
Yet ·Brutus ·says ·he ·was ·ambitious; ⌐
And ·Brutus ·is ·an ·honourable ·man. ⌐
You ·all ·did ·see ·that ·on ·the ·Lupercal ⌐
I ·thrice ·presented ·him ·a ·kingly ·crown, ⌐
Which ·he ·did ·thrice ·refuse: ·was ·this ·ambition? ⌐
Yet ·Brutus ·says ·he ·was ·ambitious; ⌐
And, ·sure, ·he ·is ·an ·honourable ·man. ⌐
I ·speak ·not ·to ·disprove ·what ·Brutus ·spoke, ⌐
But ·here ·I ·am ·to ·speak ·what ·I ·do ·know. ⌐
You ·all ·did ·love ·him ·once, ·not ·without ·cause: ⌐
What ·cause ·withholds ·you ·then, ·to ·mourn ·for ·him? ⌐
O ·judgment! ·thou ·art ·fled ·to ·brutish ·beasts, ⌐
And ·men ·have ·lost ·their ·reason. ·Bear ·with ·me; ⌐
My ·heart ·is ·in ·the ·coffin ·there ·with ·Caesar, ⌐
And ·I ·must ·pause ·till ·it ·come ·back ·to ·me.
```

Figure 2.4 Excerpt of Marc Antony's address from Shakespeare's *Julius Caesar*. *Source:* Based on *Julius Caesar,* Act III Scene II by William Shakespeare.

Table 2.3 Example Parse Result for the First Line of Mark Antony Oration

Noun	pronoun	verb	adverb	adjective	article	space	punctuation	EOL
Friends	me	lend				X	;	X
Romans	your							
Countrymen								
Ears								

romans are not confused as different terms simply because one word-term begins with a capitalization and another does not.

▨ **Parts of speech.** The value of a parser is to recognize various parts of speech. Key functions are used to determine the subject of a sentence and the treatment – often called a predicate – that is typically signaled by a verb. Because the first sentence is a form of expression (sometimes called an *oration*) the ultimate subject is hidden so here the parser must recognize that the phrase is being addressed to "friends, Romans, and countrymen" who are then populated as the subject of the sentence as nouns. Brutus and Caesar will later be recognized as named entities.

Often nouns and modifiers are often paired together. For example, we may have a "clock" to tell the time and will recognize that an "alarm clock" is a particular kind of clock. Here, "alarm clock" is a noun group. Similarly, in this passage there is the noun group "honourable man."

▨ **Transform.** With transformation we apply synonyms and other mappings or perhaps perform operations to express a negative as a positive and so on. As a simple example, imagine we have a function that replaces the phrase "lend me your ears" with a simpler expression such as "listen to me." We might also want to change the intention expressed by the subordinate phrase ". . . not to praise him" with the phrase that reflects that orator's (true) intention " . . . and to praise him." Multiple replacements of this kind can have a significant outcome in global document sentiment and mood measurements.

- **Taxonomy.** Taxonomies and typologies are classification structures where meta data that describes an entry is used to replace the entry itself.

- **Weight.** We usually weight terms in a document collection (*corpus*) to facilitate calculations and retrieval; for example, we may use term frequency (TF) calculation to normalize terms by dividing the frequency of a term by the total number of terms in a document.

Normalize here is used in the sense that frequencies are adjusted so that both frequent and infrequent terms are presented on a similar scale. There are 262 unique terms in the oration shown here. Brutus occurs 9 times and Romans or Rome occurs twice. The TF for Brutus is therefore 9/262 ➜ 0.034. The TF for Rome is 2/262 ➜ 0.007. Logarithms are often applied to term weights, as this approach tends to reduce the extreme influence of large numbers.

- Frequency weights work with the term frequency itself.
- Binary. This weight is either 1 or 0 and indicates whether or not a term is in a given document.
- $\text{Log}_n(2)$ of every frequency plus 1 is taken. Log weights lessen to effect of a single word that is repeated many times.
- None. All weights are set to 1.
- Term weights based on the document collection. In addition to TF, illustrated above, the following weights are sometimes calculated:
  - Entropy calculates the value of entropy (discussed in an earlier chapter). This assigns a higher weight to infrequent terms so emphasizes words that occur in few documents.
  - Inverse document frequency (IDF) is calculated as log (total number of documents / number of documents with term t in it). In our collection, Brutus occurs in 9 of the 262 documents so the inverse document frequency is calculated as $\log(262/9)$ ➜ 1.4.

TF x IDF emphasizes the inverse document frequency by multiplying it by the global frequency. In our case, TF for Brutus multiplied by the IDF is 0.034 * 1.4 ➜ 0.05.

Table 2.4 Internal Representation of Text Products.

Term	Role	Freq	numdocs
caesar	N	8	8
honourable man	nlpNounGroup	5	5
brutus	PN	9	9
honourable	N	5	5
ambitious	A	5	5
man	N	10	7

INTERNAL REPRESENTATION AND TEXT PRODUCTS

By default, the text processor will filter out low-frequency word-terms. This is illustrated in Table 2.4.

So, while the Mark Antony oration has a total of 130 unique terms, when the frequency filter is applied, there are only six terms ("men" and "man" are associated automatically as the same term).

Representation

The word-term occurrence and the document number are normally stored as a word x document representation.

The first few lines of the oration would be stored internally, as shown in Table 2.5.

This term by document representation now becomes the major input to a range of matrix-based statistical/numerical approaches that are widely shared across a range of quantitative analytics processes in general.

We can compare this with earlier text products (see Table 2.6).

By visual inspection of the term co-occurrence, we can see that documents 10 and 11 are most similar while 2 and 6 are most dissimilar to both documents 10 and 11. Through simple visual inspection, we see that one set of documents discusses "Brutus" and "honourable," whereas the other set of documents discuss "Caesar" and "ambitious."

Table 2.5 Terms by Document Word Frequency

		caesar	honourable man	brutus	honourable	ambitious	man
1	Friends, Romans, countrymen, lend me your ears;						
2	I come to bury Caesar, not to praise him.	x					
3	The evil that men do lives after them;						x
4	The good is oft interred with their bones;						
5	So let it be with Caesar. The noble Brutus	x		x			
6	Hath told you Caesar was ambitious:	x				x	
7	If it were so, it was a grievous fault,						
8	And grievously hath Caesar answer'd it.	x		x			
9	Here, under leave of Brutus and the rest—						
10	For Brutus is an honourable man;		x	x	x		x
11	So are they all, all honourable men—		x		x		x
12	Come I to speak in Caesar's funeral.	x					
13	He was my friend, faithful and just to me:						
14	But Brutus says he was ambitious;			x		x	
15	And Brutus is an honourable man.		x	x	x		x

Table 2.6 Term by Document Representation

	1	2	3	4	5	6	7	8	9	10	11	12	13	14	15
caesar		X			X	X		X				X			
honourable man										X	X				X
brutus				X		X		X						X	X
honourable										X	X				X
ambitious						X								X	
man			X							X	X				X

NOTES

i. A. Azevedo, and M. Santos, *KDD, SEMMA and CRISP-DM: A Parallel Overview*, IADIS European Conf. Data Mining, July 24–26 (Amsterdam, Netherlands: IADIS, 2008), 182–185.

ii. SAS Institute Inc. *Machine Learning Using SAS® Viya®* (Cary, NC: SAS Institute Inc., 2020).

iii. J.A. Cox and R. Albright, The Wondrous New tmCooccur SAS® Cloud Analytic Services (CAS) Action and Some of Its Many Uses. *SAS Global Forum, Paper 3295-2019* (Cary, NC: SAS Institute Inc., 2019).

iv. Poetry Foundation, www.poetryfoundation.org/poems/56968/speech-friends-romans-countrymen-lend-me-your-ears (accessed June 1, 2020).

CHAPTER **3**

Text Data Source Capture

TEXT MINING DATA SOURCE ASSEMBLY

Text document assembly is almost always embedded in a larger data assembly task. As we identify and tap into various text and data sources, it is typical in a multilingual world to verify and validate that we are correctly reading the text data according to how it has been encoded. When we are dealing with English-language, Latin scripts, and embedded content, we are dealing with compact representations that can be captured in standard ASCII. Increasingly, in an era of global formats it is important to ensure all types of textual data – including formal language logograms and more informal emoticons. Usually, this means turning on the input encoding to a more robust format than standard American ASCII and to use a format such as UCS-8, for example.

The inclusion of written text symbols in standard alphabetic and often pictographic form presents an additional layer of complexity beyond the collection of metric or numerical data.

Use Case: Accessing Text from SAS Conference Proceedings

There were two successive SAS conference presentations in 2012 and 2013.[i] The 2013 presentation incorporates and extends the earlier results and so serves as an instructive use case on using text analytics approaches to capture and analyze text data. The 2013 use case deals with capturing and summarizing conference presentations throughout the entire history of SAS at that time. Here we take a look at how the text data was captured and provide a brief illustration of the types of summary reports that were produced.

SAS conference proceedings taken from the annual SAS user conference from inception in 1976 through 2012 were analyzed. Proceedings from the original SAS User Group International – SUGI – from 1976 to 2006 were included, as were proceedings from SAS Global Forum (SGF) – from 2007 to 2012. At the time of these analyses, there were over 37 years of data for all SAS conferences. The annual conference had grown from an initial attendance of 206 in 1976 to over 3,000 attendees at the time of the analyses.

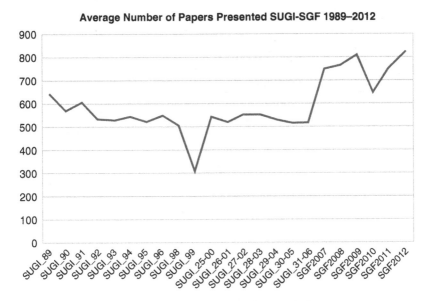

Figure 3.1 Average number of papers at SUGI-SGF 1989–2012.
Source: B. deVille.

As shown in Figure 3.1, from the late 1980s to 2012, there were, on average, a little over 600 papers presented at the annual SUGI/ SGF conference. Clearly, there is a lot of content to analyze and, just as clearly, text automation would make the job of summarizing the content more tractable than relying on human readers.

The papers given at each conference have been captured in annual proceedings. Until recently, most of these papers were only available as print publications handed out to users who attended the conference. This is a common conference practice. In 2011, the SAS Global Users Group launched and completed a project to digitize, scan, and index the historical collection of conference papers. This project resulted in a digital repository of 9,134 papers.[ii] This repository was the focus of this research and constituted the data set. Retrieving content from an archived corpus of SUGI-SGF presentations was the front-end part of a joint analysis conducted with Lavalley and Bedford and presented at the SGF 2013.[iii]

Table 3.1 Format of the Conference Proceedings Input File

Field	Field Description
Conference	Title of the conference
Year	Year of conference
Stream	Conference stream; data, applications, programming, etc.
Paperid	Unique document identifier
Title	Title of the paper or presentation
Author	Author(s) of document
Award	Conference awards, if any
Link	url locator link to permanent, scannable, document location

Text Data Capture Process

All original conference material from the period 1976–2012 was downloaded in a temporary data set. This data set contains a list of file locations that point to the papers and presentations and papers that were available on the archive at the time of the analysis. There were approximately 13,600 documents available for the analysis. Table 3.1 shows the headings they were organized under.

This set of file names can be used as an input parameter to a file scraping facility. In our case, we used the %TMFilter macro.[iv] This macro reads original source file in .pdf format and then loads the scanned and parsed text into an output data set in SAS format.

The first record of the file dates to the SUGI 1 conference in 1976:

SUGI01
1976
<blank>
sugi76.002-1976
GENERAL LINEAR MODEL PROCEDURE
James W Goodnight
<blank>
http://www.sascommunity.org/sugi/SUGI76/Sugi-76-02 Goodnight.pdf

The last record (number 13,627) is as follows:

SGF2012
2012
Travel, Hospitality and Entertainment
sgf2012.384-2012
Factoring Upgrades into Overbooking Decisions for Hotels and Casinos
Tugrul Sanli
<blank>
http://support.sas.com/resources/papers/proceedings12/384-2012.pdf

The %TMFilter program has settings to limit the number of characters read from a file (and, in cases of long files to read past the normal 32,767 character limit used by the macro). The Shaik et al. approach used programmatic settings and PERL expressions in the %SAS1976 macro to ensure that only the abstract for the paper was captured. The Lavalley et al.[v] approach captured all presentation text, using the macro %run_tmfilter_all.

Individual files were combined to create a global text analysis file for the respective approaches. Shaik et al.[vi] concatenated all the files in the %SAS1976 macro. Lavalley et al.[vii] concatenated the files in the %write_all.sas macro. A subset of documents, representing the most recent years from 1989 to 2012, is used for this latter analysis.

The %tm_filter macro is used to translate all the original source files into a standard text format. A typical tm_filter instruction is as follows:

```
libname ss_text "C:\SUGI_etc\SUGI_89\text";
%tmfilter (dataset=ss_text.docs_89,
dir=C:\SUGI_etc\SUGI_89,
numchars=32767, ext=.pdf);
```

Here, the macro points to the original file stored in C:\SUGI_etc\ SUGI_89 that is contained in .pdf format. The resulting text file is stored in the *docs_89* file.

Text	Conference	Name	Year
A SAS Software Integrated System for Technical Information Management Ronald R. MacDonald, Roy F. Weston Inc. Shi-Tao Yeh, Roy F. Weston Inc. Antnony Kreamer(Roy F". weston Inc. Stephen J. Medvid, Roy F4 weston Inc. ABSTRACT This paper describes a menu driven technical information system developed	SUGI_89	MacDonald.pdf	1989
RETRO-ENGINEERING A SAS? REPORTING SYSTEM FRONTEND Brent Turner, City of New York Th* Financial Information Services Agency (FISA) o-f the Citv of New York has been created as a requirement for federal subsidies Used to assist the City in meeting its financial obligatians. These subsidies had initially	SUGI_89	SUGI 89-130 Turner.pdf	1989
● ● ●		● ● ●	
Paper 435-2012 Combating Insurance Claims Fraud James Ruotolo, SAS Institute Inc. ABSTRACT This paper will discuss how to Recognize and Reduce Opportunistic and Organized Insurance Claims Fraud. Come and learn about the features of the SAS? Fraud Framework. No paper was submitted for publication in the	SGF2012	435-2012.pdf	2012

Figure 3.2 Example snippet of text input to conference proceedings analysis.
Source: B. deVille.

The %writeall macro was designed to take all the original text documents and create a single, concatenated input file suitable for text analysis.

```
%macro writeall;
libname ss_all "C:\SUGI_etc\data";
/* Main loop                                          */
%do i=1 %to &numyrs;
%let thelib =%left(%scan(&libs,&i,' '));
%let toread=%left(%scan(&dsets,&i,' '));
libname ss_text "&thelib";
/* Read each input file                               */
data &toread;
set ss_text.&toread (keep = text uri name);
run;
/* Create the concatenated main file */
proc append base=ss_all.all_text data=&toread. force;
run;

%end;
%mend writeall;
```

Figure 3.2 provides a condensed example (snippet) of what the combined records from the final concatenation process look like.

CONSUMING LINGUISTICS TEXT PRODUCTS

We have seen how the text mining parse capability allows us to identify various parts of speech (noun, verb, and so on), as well as specific entities (e.g., person, location). As an illustration of abstracting higher dimensional products that are based on parsed text products, let's focus on parts of speech that can serve as subjects of a sentence – typically a noun or noun phrase. In this example, we will select only noun phrases from the text corpus that we put together for the selected time period of 1989–2012. Our intent is to derive a high-level summary of significant subjects to serve as a classification of papers presented at the various conferences.

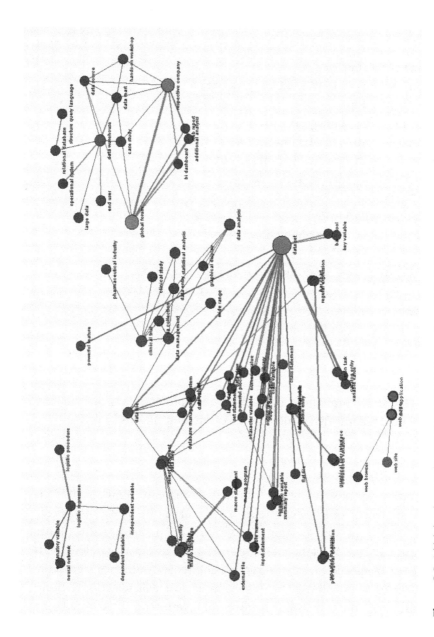

Figure 3.3 A high-level semantic map of conference proceedings, 1989–2012.
Source: B. deVille.

From these noun phrases, we used the Association Node (SAS Institute, 2020) calculation to produce a network diagram that will serve as a *semantic map* to describe the overall content of SGF-SUGI proceedings during our target 1989–2012 time period. The Association Node will map linkages between noun phrases on a document by document basis. When strong linkages between noun phrases are discovered, as shown in the link diagram map in Figure 3.3, we have an indication of which noun phrases associate together. These strong associations of noun phrases can serve as proxies for strong subject matter themes. As a methodological note, we might pause to notice the relationship between association maps, network diagrams, and the co-occurrence analytics that we use to drive higher dimensional products like text clusters and topics. The founders of Google, Sergei Brin and Larry Page, made a similar observation in the development of the Pagerank algorithm that was an initial basis for the highly successful Google search engine.[viii]

NOTES

i. Z. Shaik, S. Garla, and G. Chakraborty, *SAS® Since 1976: An Application of Text Mining to Reveal Trends*, SAS Global Forum, Paper 135-2012 (Cary, NC: SAS Institute Inc., 2012). https://support.sas.com/resources/papers/proceedings13/135-2012.pdf.

ii. R. La Valley, L. Jansen, and K. Lafler, *Recovering SAS® User Group Proceedings for the SAS® Community* (Cary, NC: SAS Institute Inc., 2013).

iii. R. La Valley, D. Bedford, and B. deVille, B. *A Tale of Two SAS® Technologies: Generating Maps of Topical Coverage and Linkages in SAS User Conference Papers*. SAS Global Forum, Paper 102-2013 (Cary, NC: SAS Institute Inc., 2013). https://support.sas.com/resources/papers/proceedings13/102-2013.pdf.

iv. SAS Institute Inc., *SAS® Text Miner 15.1: Reference Help* (Cary, NC: SAS Institute Inc., 2018).

v. La Valley, Jansen, and Lafler, *Recovering SAS® User Group Proceedings for the SAS® Community*.

vi. Shaik, Garla, and Chakraborty, *SAS® Since 1976*.

vii. La Valley, Jansen, and Lafler, *Recovering SAS® User Group Proceedings for the SAS® Community*.

viii. S. Brin, and L. Page, "The Anatomy of a Large-Scale Hypertextual Web Search Engine," *Computer Networks* 30 (1998): 107–117.

CHAPTER **4**

Document
Content and
Characterization

AUTHORSHIP ANALYTICS: EARLY TEXT INDICATORS AND MEASURES

Text analytics have long been used to resolve questions on author attribution and is one area that predates modern higher-dimensional, computational methods. One of the earliest examples is the work of Mosteller and Wallace[i] to identify the authorship of 12 disputed essays in *The Federalist Papers*. Between the years 1787 and 1788, Alexander Hamilton, John Jay, and James Madison wrote 85 expositions, or essays, designed to help get the US Constitution ratified, published anonymously under the pseudonym "Publius." The authorship of certain of *The Federalist Papers* was ambiguous, as both Hamilton and Madison produced lists that claimed some of the same papers.

Function Words as Indicators

Initially, the authors used sentence lengths (number of words per sentence) to distinguish authorship. Later researchers, for example, Fung,[ii] used function words (FW) (Table 4.1) to form a hyperplane between two sets of documents. This latter technique is also used by one of the psychological researchers[iii] taken up later in this chapter.

Fung's approach is based on computing the relative frequencies (number of occurrences per 1000 words of the text) of the 70 function words (Table 4.1). The training data set consists of authorship as the target field concatenated with 70 predictor fields that consist of the relative frequencies of the 70 function words. The Fung analysis resulted in a hyperplane that classified all the training data correctly. The final hyperplane, based on *tenfold cross validation*, found three optimal predictors – to, upon, and would. The 12 ambiguous papers ended up on the Madison side of the hyperplane.

Table 4.1 Function Words

1 a	15 do	29 is	43 or	57 this
2 all	16 down	30 it	44 our	58 to
3 also	17 even	31 its	45 shall	59 up
4 an	18 every	32 may	46 should	60 upon
5 and	19 for	33 more	47 so	61 was
6 any	20 from	34 must	48 some	62 were
7 are	21 had	35 my	49 such	63 what
8 as	22 has	36 no	50 than	64 when
9 at	23 have	37 not	51 that	65 which
10 be	24 her	38 now	52 the	66 who
11 been	25 his	39 of	53 their	67 will
12 but	26 if	40 on	54 then	68 with
13 by	27 in	41 one	55 there	69 would
14 can	28 into	42 only	56 things	70 your

Beyond Function Words

An article in the *Journal of the American Society for Information Science and Technology*[iv] provides an overview of the various methods that have been found useful in authorship applications:

- **Syntax and parts of speech (POS).** These indicators use frequencies of short sequences of parts-of-speech (POS), or combinations of POS and other classes of words, as a simple method for approximating syntactic features. These features are then used as predictors of the target field.

- **Functional lexical taxonomies (SFL).** These include function words, combined with parts of speech based on systemic functional linguistics (SFL).[v] These taxonomies include various parts of speech, as well as function words (e.g., articles, auxiliary verbs, conjunctions, prepositions, pronouns).

- ▦ **Content words (CW).** This approach looks for particular content words (e.g., one author might use the words "start" and "large" whereas another might use "begin" and "big").
- ▦ **Character *n*-grams (CNG).** In addition to word or term *n*-grams, combinations of adjacent character *n*-grams are also suggested as being useful in predicting authorship. Character *n*-grams are assumed to be language-independent.

A summary of the measures proposed are presented in Table 4.2.

A recent offshoot of the character *n*-gram is a more generic *n*-gram capability built by Google.[vi]

Words and Word Forms as Psychological Artifacts

James Pennebaker has pioneered a unique form of text analytics that looks at words and term use, parts of speech, and style of expression as indicators of underlying psychological states and social processes, so rather than make inferences about the author based on linguistic measures, we make inferences about the author based on the written expressions produced by the author.

In a broad sense, Pennebaker takes authored documents as free-form instruments that tell us about the underlying psychology of the author just as psychometric interviews and psychometric response scales are used to identify various facets of individual psychology.

Table 4.2 Feature Types and Machine Learning Methods

FW	A list of 512 function words, including conjunctions, prepositions, pronouns, modal verbs, determiners, and numbers (purely stylistic).
POS	Identify 38 part-of-speech unigrams and 1,000 most common bigrams using a part-of-speech tagger (purely stylistic).
SFL	Construct SFL tags using conjunctions, prepositions, pronouns, and modal verbs.
CW	Identify the 1,000 words with highest information gain in the training corpus among the 10,000 most common words in the corpus.
CNG	Identify the 1,000 character trigrams with highest information gain in the training corpus among the 10,000 most common trigrams in the corpus.

Source: Based on M. Koppel, J. Schler, and S. Argamon, "Computational methods in authorship attribution," *Journal of the American Society for Information Science and Technology* 60 (1) (2009): 9–26. https://doi.org/10.1002/asi.20961.

During the course of his research on the role of expressive writing on psychological outcomes he developed an approach to the analytic treatment of text called the *Linguistic Inquiry and Word Count* (LIWC),[vii] The resulting program outputs the percentage of words in a given text that fall into a range over 80 linguistic (e.g., first-person singular pronouns, conjunctions), psychological (e.g., anger, achievement), and topical (e.g., leisure, money) categories. The categories include negative emotion words (sad, angry), positive emotion words (happy, laugh), standard function word categories (first, second, and third person pronouns, articles, prepositions), and various content categories (e.g., religion, death, occupation).

Pennebaker published a popular account of his work as *The Secret Life of Pronouns*.[viii] Pennebaker explains that, unlike traditional linguistics, his approach has roots in the structure of the human brain – specifically, the mapping between various regions of the brain and the highly social forms of expression involved in speech and communication.

The frontal lobe of the human cerebral cortex is disproportionately large compared to most other mammals. Most social and internal psychology management skills are highly dependent on a robust frontal lobe. Language and expression are also important functions of the frontal lobe. The dominant temporal lobe contains Wernicke's area. This is an area that is responsible for understanding and generating most advanced speech such as nouns, verbs, and most adjectives.

Broca's area is in the frontal node region on the dominant side of the brain (typically the left side). Damage to Broca's area results in people speaking in painfully slow, hesitating way, often devoid of function words. People with a functioning Broca's area but with a compromised Wernicke's area display a warm and fluid social style but use primarily function words, which are devoid of content. Most content is conveyed by workhorse nouns and verbs of our vocabulary. Here we can begin to see the substantial relationship between word forms and underlying brain physiology and neural tendency and capacity. In addition to the insight into content-free function words and content-laden nouns and verbs, we can look at pronouns with the understanding that pronouns require a shared understanding of the relationship between speaker and listener.

Language use and vocabulary markers demonstrated several observable patterns:

- **Deception.** Conjunctions, negations, and some prepositions are used to make important distinctions about categories. Some words are exclusion words. These include words like "but," "except," "without," and "exclude." These words tend to be associated with negations (no, not, never), and overall are associated with greater cognitive complexity.[ix] The combined use of first-person singular pronouns and exclusion words has been shown to predict honesty.

- **Demographics.** There are gender differences in the use of the majority of function words: pronouns, prepositions, articles, and auxiliary verbs. In a study of over 10,000 text files, Newman et al.[x] found that females tend to use first-person singular pronouns at a consistently higher rate than do males.

  Another large gender difference is that males' natural speech and writing contain higher rates of article and noun use, which characterizes categorization, or concrete thinking. However, females use more verbs (especially auxiliary verbs), which highlights females' relational orientation.

  Age differences in function words are also robust. Pennebaker and Stone[xi] found that as people age, they tend to use fewer first-person singular words in preference to greater first-person plural words. An analysis of their auxiliary verbs indicates that age tends to favor the use of more future tense and less past tense.

- **Categorization (and culture).** Function words that indicate categorization include articles ("a," "an," "the") that are used with nouns. Some scholars, such as Peng and Nisbett (1999),[xii] argue that Western thought from the time of the early Greeks has been highly categorical. Research by Chung and Pennebaker[xiii] shows that translations from Japanese contain fewer function words such as "a," "an," and "the" that come before nouns (categories).

A CASE STUDY IN GENDER DETECTION

Detecting and correcting gender attribution is a historically important function in data quality and, more recently, an important function in various media monitoring applications, especially in marketing applications where gender-specific product offers are made. In classical data quality applications gender is often assigned based on the registered name in the database. One technique is to cross-reference names to Social Security registration data that track common names by gender. Typically, names are drawn from Social Security card applications for births that occurred in the United States after 1879. For example, we can go to the Social Security location https://www.ssa.gov/oact/babynames/limits.html and then download one or more of the many names data sets.

This will give us information shown in Table 4.3.

For our case study, we also completed a more extensive review of the literature. Table 4.4 lists several example sources, together with an indication of the textual features that have been shown to be predictive of gender.

- **Test data.** For test data, we used comments taken from the WebMD site. Since registered users were used for the data, we had a well-populated and relatively reliable target field in order to conduct the analysis.

Table 4.3 Baby Names and Likely Gender (from US Social Security Records)

Name	Female	Name	Male
Emma	F	*John*	*M*
Olivia	F	*William*	*M*
Ava	F	*James*	*M*
Isabella	F	*Robert*	*M*
Sophia	F	*George*	*M*
Charlotte	F	*Frank*	*M*
Mia	F	*Joseph*	*M*
Amelia	F	*Charles*	*M*
Harper	F	*Edward*	*M*

Source: Based on Baby Names and Likely Gender, U.S. Social Security.

Table 4.4 Textual Features as Predictors from Research

Source	Notable Features
Miller, G.A., Newman, E.B. and Friedman E.A. (1958). Length-frequency statistics for written English. *Information and Control* 1 (4): 370–389 https://doi.org/10.1016/S0019-9958(58)90229-8.	Classic findings: function words (list from Fries) vs. content words
Roger D. Peng, Nicolas W. Hengartner (2002) Quantitative Analysis of Literary Styles. *The American Statistician* 56 (3).	Function words
Chung, C. K. and Pennebaker, J. W. (2007). The psychological function of function words. *Social Communication: Frontiers of Social Psychology (ed. K. Fiedler)*, 343–359. New York: Psychology Press.	First-person singular pronouns
	First-person plural pronouns
	Non-I pronouns
	Exclusion words (cognitive complexity)
	Objects
Shlomo Argamon. Moshe Koppel, Jonathan Fine, Anat Rachel Shimoni (2003) Gender, Genre, and Writing Style in Formal Written Texts. *Text* 23 (3): 321–346.	Relationships (social and otherwise?)
	Concrete thinking
	pronouns
	I, you, she, its
	part of speech *n*-grams
	Talkativeness
Leaper, C. and Ayres, M. (2007). A Meta-Analytic Review of Gender Variations in Adults' Language Use. *Personality and Social Psychology Review* 11(4): 328–363.	Affiliative
	Assertive
Robin T. Lakoff (1973) Language and Woman's Place. *Language in Society* 2 (1) (Apr. 1973): 45–80. http://www.jstor.org/stable/4166707 Accessed: 15/04/2009 20:06	Quantifiers {one, two, more, some} -- cardinality
	Hedge phrases (I think, kind of, I believe, it seems to me, I don't know, but ...)
	Empty adjectives: e.g., lovely, adorable, gorgeous
	Hyper-polite: e.g., would you mind ..., I'd much appreciate if ...
	Apologetic: e.g., I am very sorry, but I think that ...
	Tag questions: e.g., you don't mind, do you?

Table 4.4 (*Continued*)

Source	Notable Features
Burger, J.D., Henderson, J., Kim, G., and Zarrella, G. (2011). Discriminating Gender on Twitter. *Proceedings of the 2011 Conference on Empirical Methods in Natural Language Processing.* 1301–1309.	Exclamation points are the #1 predictor of female gender in a Tweet
	Emoticons (or subparts of emoticons) were predictive of gender
	bigrams – token

■ **Data assembly.** We ran all the comment fields from the WebMD records through a style and feature detection process that was designed to pick up the following predictive fields.

Data Product Example

Data products used in document characterization are shown in Table 4.5.

Table 4.5 Summary of Extracted Text Products Used in Document Characterization

Data Product	Example
Function words	Include personal pronouns, impersonal pronouns, prepositions, articles, conjunctions, negations, quantifiers, adverbs, auxiliary verbs e.g., *I, me, you, he, can, for, it, of, this*
I words	*I, me, mine, my*
Big words	Compute word length. Use 10% above average in a document as an indicator.
Certainty words	*absolutely, unequivocally, surely, certainly*
Hedge words	*I believe, kind of, it seems to me, I don't know but, it seems to me, I think*
Cognitive words	Words that grasp insight: *understand, know, think.* e.g., Cognitive words like *"I think that I was told about that,"* or searching for insight: *"I was told about that?"*
Social words	Any words that are related to another human being: e.g., *friendly, nice friendly, kind, pleasant, warm, genuine, honest, friendly and sincere, pleasant, welcoming, amiable, friendly and pleasant, good-natured, bubbly, lively, happy, and friendly, warm-hearted, friendly, kind, and generous,*

Table 4.5 (Continued)

Data Product	Example
Causal words	Because, reason, rationale, cause, effect, reason, rationale, impel, control, or, and, but, because, hence, therefore, since Others: who, what, where, when, why, will, can, do/does, was/were, are/is, how much/many/often/far
Concrete words	Articles, nouns, categories. Function words that indicate categorization include articles (a, an, the), which are used with nouns.
Pronouns	Primarily forms of the pronouns: I, you, he, she, it Personal, third-person pronouns (he, she) use is far greater for females than males in both fiction and nonfiction (there is a particularly striking difference for the female pronouns). It: Never personal its: Used more by males For first-person, the mean proportion of plural pronouns to overall pronouns (1 p-plu/1p) for male authors is 50.7, while for female authors it is only 42.2. Likewise, for third-person, the mean proportion of plural pronouns to overall pronouns for male authors is 20.4, while for female authors it is only 14.8. For second-person pronouns, use the proportion yourselves/(yourselves + yourself) as a proxy. For males, the mean is 6.8, while for females it is only 4.7.
Exclusive words	but, except, without, exclude
Lying	Stories that were true had more words in them and more details than those that were fake. The true stories had fewer emotion terms in them than the fakes. The true stories had fewer verbs than the fakes. Finally, the true stories had more first-person pronouns in them than the fakes.
Age	Age differences in function words are also robust. Pennebaker and Stone (2003) found that people use fewer first-person singular words and greater first-person plural words with age. Interestingly, the analysis of their auxiliary verbs indicates that people use more future tense and less past tense the older they get, suggesting a shift in focus through the aging process.

Analysis Results

Figure 4.1 shows the high-level results of the analysis of gender as a target in the WebMD data using over 30 predictor word form derivatives that have been shown to be predictive of gender (based on a representative review of studies in the literature).

Figure 4.1 shows that the top 10 predictors have substantial predictive power (as measured by the worth statistic, which measures the

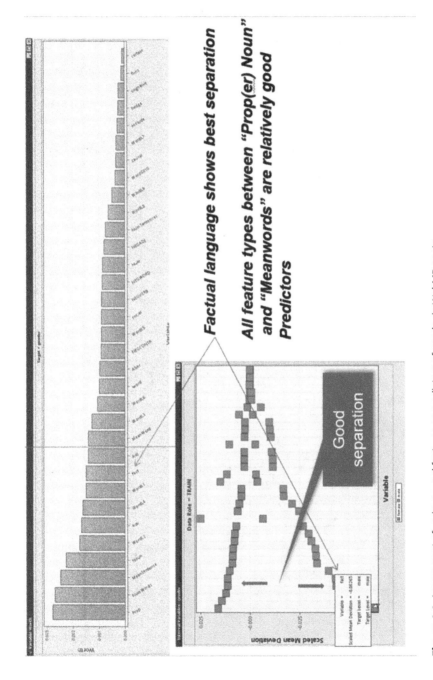

Figure 4.1 Assessment of various word features as predictors of gender in WebMD posts.
Source: B. deVille.

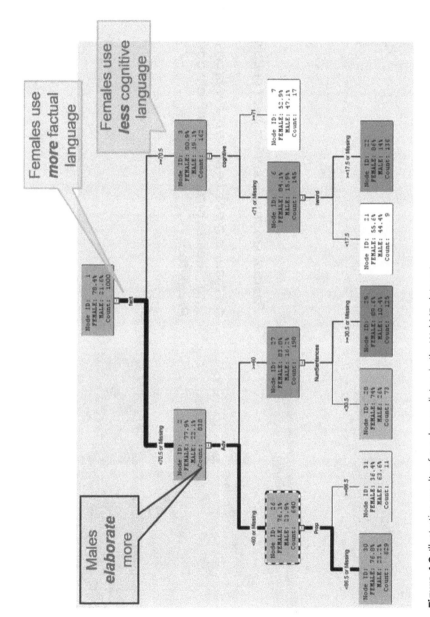

Figure 4.2 Illustrative results of gender predictors in the WebMD data set.
Source: B. deVille.

54

probability of chi-squared formed by the table of the target frequencies by predictor categories). With this data set, these predictors are:

- Prevalence of proper nouns
- Average number of words
- Average sentence length
- Prevalence of nouns
- Prevalence of words of length 2
- Prevalence of adjectives
- Prevalence of words of length 4
- Factual words
- Prevalence of adjectives

In Figure 4.2, we combine these simple two-way relationships to show the combined effect of these predictors on characterizing male versus female authors.

Here, we see that one of the strongest predictors of gender of author is whether they use factual language: females tend to use more factual language. Among those who tend to use more factual language, the males tend to use more cognitive language. Among those who use less factual language, males tend to elaborate more (as shown by the relative prevalence of adverbial word forms).

This is preliminary, explorative work and is far from definitive. This illustration is designed to illustrate how the word form predictors can be calculated and how they could be used in an analysis.

SUMMARIZATION AND DISCOURSE ANALYSIS

A significant amount of text processing involves reading documents and producing written and numerical summaries. Linguistic processes are particularly well adapted to this kind of task. We present an example taken from work presented by deVille and Wolff;[xiv] here the authors show how linguistic processing can be used to simplify and automate a number of the manual text analytic tasks. The main tool for linguistic processing and information extraction (IE) in SAS is implementation of the LITI processor, which stands for *language interpretation for textual information.* More information on the LITI syntax can be found in the *Visual Text Analytics User's Guide.*^{xv} Two scenarios are described:

1. Hospitalization histories – useful in processing insurance claims – are produced.

2. Reactions to drugs in the general population (subsequent to forma clinical trials).

Text analytics in the reporting domains of health and life sciences often involves the analysis and preparation of data for various pharmacovigilance applications such as Periodic Safety Update Report (PSUR) and the Vaccine Adverse Event Reporting System (VAERS),^{xvi} as well as for the collection and summarization of treatment histories for medical procedures and hospitalization histories.

Another example is the text analytic nature of pharmacovigilance:

- Much of the data – in the range of 80 percent – is unstructured.
- Linguistic approaches, such as NLP, are required to identify drug treatments, procedures, and effects.
- Several analytic approaches that involve numerical manipulation of various kinds are required to identify sums of treatment events, ranges of dosage, onset date of conditions, and so on.
- Advanced linguistics, coupled with the numerical assessment of ranges and differences, are required to detect such nuances as "somewhat elevated" and "10 percent increase."
- A few elementary operations can serve as building blocks, which can be combined to transform raw inputs into semi-finished information products fit for rapid human review and storage for subsequent retrieval and publication.

Elementary Operations as Building Blocks to Results

The basic techniques in report construction involve the construction of facilities that can:

- Detect events (and associated timing and other details).
- Detect linked objects (and associated attributes).

Event and Object Recognition and Summarization

Event and object recognition are shown in Figure 4.3. This example treatment summary is taken from preparatory work in the application of text analytics to medical records (in-patient hospitalization records analysis). The basic content of the summary has been identified by scanning hospitalization admission and treatment files (merged together using a patient identifier field).

The earliest date on file, coupled with an analysis of the "Notes" field, shown in Figure 4.3, allows us to establish the admission date.

As shown in the following steps, text input files can be scanned for varieties of medically relevant terminology such as "treatment" and "diagnosis." Elementary operations such as counting and associated with dates that are detected can then be used to assemble the elements of a textual report.

1. The notes file is scanned for interesting text combinations and, as shown in Figure 4.4, a scanned output file can be constructed.

2. An analysis of the "Diagnosis" field allows us to establish a provisional medical diagnosis.

3. Scanning the events records allows us to count and sum the number of treatments. For example, as shown on Figure 4.5,

---

```
Diagnosis of Metastatic ovarian cancer 7/19/2006
Promoted to Longitudinal Case Management 7/24/2006
Diagnosis of Benign hypertension 7/28/2006
Multiple treatments of surgery 8/2/2006 and chemotherapy 8/16/2006 - 1/7/2007
Patient re-admitted 7/24 2006.
Treatment of intravenous medications (4 times) dates 12/24/2007 -- 1/06/2008 duration 12 days.
Treatment of chemotherapy (7 times) dates xx/yy -- 01/02/2008 duration 14 months.
Treatment of abdominal catheter placement date 01/02/2008.
Referred to the ICA for management of inpatient admission
Medical Director note. cancer of ovary mets to liver. peritonitis, ascites, abd pain. Date 12/23
Medical Director note. cancer of ovary mets to liver. peritonitis, ascites, abd pain. Date 01/02
discharged to inpatient hospice date 1/10
admission -- discharge 19 days
Patient expired Date 1/13
hospice admission -- patient expired 3 days
```

Figure 4.3 Example of medical notes used as input.
Source: B. deVille.

	descriptor	Result	date
1	Treatment:	surgery	8/2/2006
2	Diagnosis:	surgery	8/2/2006
3	Treatment:	chemotherapy	8/17/2006
4	Diagnosis:	chemotherapy	8/17/2006
5	Diagnosis:	chemotherapy	8/17/2006
6	Treatment:	chemotherapy	8/16/2006
7	Diagnosis:	chemotherapy	8/16/2006
8	Diagnosis:	chemotherapy	8/16/2006
9	Treatment:	chemotherapy	8/16/2006
10	Diagnosis:	chemotherapy	8/16/2006
11	Diagnosis:	Benign hypertension	7/28/2006
12	Quarter:	3rd Quarter	7/27/2007
13	Quarter:	3rd Quarter	7/26/2007
14	Admission:	Patient re-admitted}	7/26/2007
15	Event:	ICA Referral generated	7/24/2007
16	Event:	Promoted to Longitudinal	7/24/2006
17	Diagnosis:	Metastatic ovarian cance	7/23/2006
18	Diagnosis:	Metastatic ovarian cance	7/19/2006
19	Event:	Patient discharged home	2/16/2007
20	Diagnosis:	intravenous medication	12/24/2007
21	Diagnosis:	intravenous medication	12/24/2007
22	Diagnosis:	intravenous medication	12/24/2007
23	Diagnosis:	intravenous medication	12/24/2007

Figure 4.4 Result of text parsing to match notable document features for summary and tabulation.
Source: B. deVille.

we establish that this patient has had multiple admissions so can produce a notation to that effect.

4. As shown in Figure 4.6, the "Notes" field on the latest data entry allows us to establish the disposition of the patient and associated date.

These presentations are supported by the operation of linguistic and computational procedures that are a standard part of SAS text analytics. Some of the more important procedures are discussed below.

Diagnosis of Metastatic ovarian cancer 7/19/2006

Promoted to Longitudinal Case Management 7/24/2006

Diagnosis of Benign hypertension 7/28/2006

Multiple treatments of surgery 8/2/2006 and chemotherapy 8/16/2006 - 1/7/2007

Patient re-admitted 7/24 2006.

Treatment of intravenous medications (4 times) dates 12/24/2007 -- 1/06/2008 duration 12 days.

Treatment of chemotherapy (7 times).dates xx/yy -- 01/02/2008 duration 14 months.

Treatment of abdominal catheter placement date 01/02/2008.

Referred to the ICA for management of inpatient admission

Medical Director note. **cancer of ovary mets to liver.** peritonitis, ascites, abd pain. Date 12/23

Medical Director note. **cancer of ovary mets to liver.** peritonitis, ascites, abd pain. Date 01/02

discharged to inpatient hospice date 1/10

admission -- discharge 19 days

Patient expired Date 1/13

Figure 4.5 Pro-forma text summary production based on the structured textual summary record.
Source: B. deVille.

Categories, Concepts, and Event-Object Summarization and Arithmetic

The Text Analytics tool set enables us to identify a number of situations that arise in PSUR report production.

Category Identification

Figure 4.7 shows how SAS textual content categorization functionality identifies the condition (category) reported in the text. As shown in the figure, "Respiratory Diseases" is identified as one of the

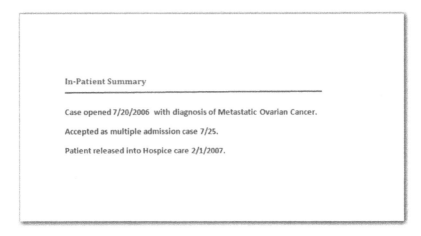

In-Patient Summary

Case opened 7/20/2006 with diagnosis of Metastatic Ovarian Cancer.

Accepted as multiple admission case 7/25.

Patient released into Hospice care 2/1/2007.

Figure 4.6 Example summary record (hospitalization).
Source: B. deVille.

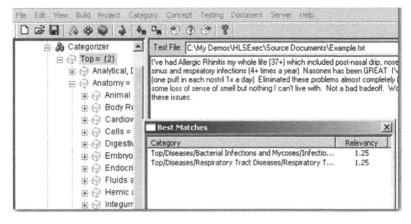

Figure 4.7 Example of text analytics categorization.
Source: B. deVille.

primary characteristics of this condition report (here, relevancy is calculated at 1.25).

Figure 4.7 provides an example of how various diseases and other medical conditions can be defined and detected. Many medical taxonomies, such as the MeSH Medical Subject Headings (US National

Library of Medicine), are automatically updated by standards bodies and are available for use in applications.

Concept Identification and Conceptual Extraction

Figure 4.8 provides an example of how a regular expression can be used to identify a date field in the form of mm/dd/yy. As shown here, the SAS text analytics functionally employ a standard Perl regular expression syntax. Here, the Perl regular expression for date is coded as [0-9]+\/[0-9]+\/[0-9]+ (indicating we should scan the incoming text stream for three sets of one or more numeric characters separated by a "/" character).[xvii]

Event-Object Summarization and Arithmetic

Once the incoming stream of text is identified, the results can be placed in a data store that can then be manipulated using standard SAS products such as *SAS Enterprise Guide*.

Figure 4.9 shows the relationship between fields of data and the resulting text summary. Here, numerous "chemotherapy" diagnoses are detected (along with the associated dates), so the text summary reads:

"Multiple treatments of . . . chemotherapy between 8/2/2006 and . . . ." (The example shown here also includes summaries for surgeries and the associated date ranges.)

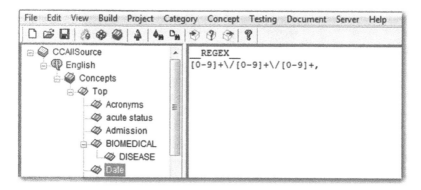

Figure 4.8 Example date definition (using standard Perl regular expressions).
Source: B. deVille.

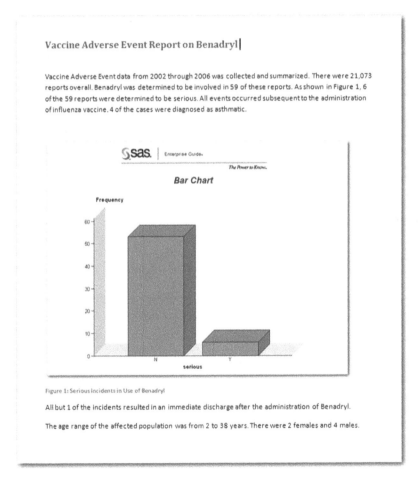

Figure 4.9 Illustration of the relationship between extracted fields of data and associated report fragment.
Source: B. deVille.

Figure 4.10 Example report applying approach to VAERS data.
Source: B. deVille.

Example of Elementary Operators

The three elementary operations used with in-patient records are categories, concepts, and event-object summarization and arithmetic. The operations are readily generalizable to other collections of data that have either text fields with structure or which have fields of data that can be re-formed in a structured fashion. An example is shown in Figure 4.10. Each element of this report – for example, event outcome – is either a field in the analysis or is an object that can be detected with linguistic scanning.

The associated project that produces this result is illustrated in Figure 4.11.

All results were produced using one of the three elementary operations: categories, concepts, and event-object summarization and arithmetic. In this case, the output is routed through a Microsoft Word engine to produce Word display format.

Other Elementary Operations

As shown above, event detection and object recognition are key features to the successful quantitative summarization of descriptive records.

Other required operations, illustrated below, include fact extraction, sentiment identification, and conditional inference.

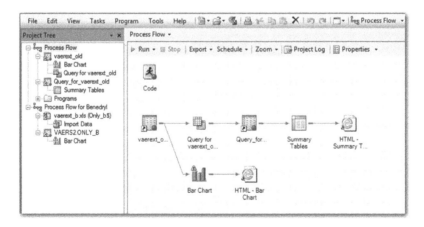

Figure 4.11 A Process flow diagram for VAERS report.
Source: B. deVille.

FACT EXTRACTION

SAS text analytics is capable of extracting specific information in context (facts), as shown in Figure 4.12. Here we detect a *loss of sense of smell* that is associated with the use of the drug. The expression to identify this fact hinges on the phrase "loss of sense of smell." The syntax of the expression is shown in Figure 4.12.

As shown in Figure 4.13, we have an overall positive assessment of the drug ("Nasonex has been GREAT"). Sentiment analysis is included in the suite of SAS text analytics products and is specifically equipped to:

- Identify various attributes of assessment.
- Identify positive, negative, and neutral emotional charge associated with the specific attribute.
- Create an overall sentiment score that depends on the weight of the attributes and associated emotional charge.

I've had Allergic Rhinitis my whole life (37+ years) which included post-nasal drip, nose, ear and chest congestion, recurrent sinus and respiratory infections (4+ times a year). Nasonex has been GREAT. I've been taking this for four months now (one puff each nostril 1x a day). Eliminated these problems almost completely (knock on wood). I've noticed I've had some loss of sense of smell but nothing I can't live with. Not a bad tradeoff. Would recommend this to anyone with these issues.

Fact Extraction Set-up

- *PREDICATE: DRUG_SIDE_EFFECT* (drug, side-effect):
  (ORD,(DIST_30, "_drug{DRUG)",
                  "OBSERVATION-KEYWORD",
                  "_side-effect{SIDE-EFFECT}"))
  ARGUMENT: drug = Nasonex
  ARGUMENT: side-effect = loss of sense of smell

Figure 4.12 Fact extraction (information in context).
Source: B. deVille.

Sentiment Extraction

I've had Allergic Rhinitis my whole life (37+ years) which included post-nasal drip, nose, ear and chest congestion, recurrent sinus and respiratory infections (4+ times a year). Nasonex has been GREAT. I've been taking this for four months now (one puff each nostril 1x a day). Eliminated these problems almost completely (knock on wood). I've noticed I've had some loss of sense of smell but nothing I can't live with. Not a bad tradeoff. Would recommend this to anyone with these issues.

- **Sentiment Analysis**
    - o POSITIVE (Nasonex has been GREAT)
    - o POSITIVE (Eliminated these problems almost completely)
    - o NEUTRAL (Not a bad tradeoff)
    - o POSITIVE (Would recommend this to anyone with these issues)

Figure 4.13 Example of sentiment extraction.
Source: B. deVille.

Conditional Inference

Conditional inference is based on a standard predicate rule structure, which, in turn, is based on first-order logic.[xviii] This logic allows us to make both formal and informal inferences based on logical relationships. Figure 4.14 provides an example of a predicate rule that identifies a dose when two text conditions are found in the same textual context.

In the example shown in Figure 4.14, we see that the detection syntax can be set up to look for instances of "dose reductions" and "dose-dependent side effects." Taken in the context of other information, such as disease condition or brand name, this enables us to populate the record with the associated field.

Deployment

These forms of elementary operations that we have reviewed here are useful for automating a wide range of medical scenarios.

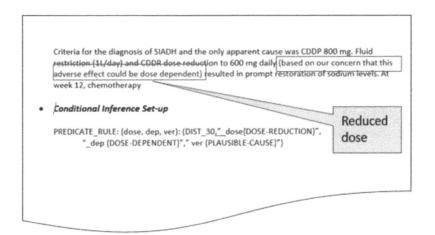

Figure 4.14 Example of conditional inference.
Source: B. deVille.

Typical output is a case summary as shown in Figure 4.15 that presents a resume of the case. The information is typically presented in two to three paragraphs (often with an associated numerical table or Excel worksheet). This is information that is otherwise normally contained in several pages of text.

In order to produce a good summary of this example case narrative, the software has to identify the terms that are highlighted in Figure 4.16. These include chemical compositions, drug names, diagnoses, as well as potential side effects. The technical components of these recognition requirements are readily identified using taxonomies such as the MeSH taxonomy referred to earlier.

As shown above, the recognition features are examples of category, concept, or object-event recognition operations.

As we continue on the examination of the case narrative, we can see other information – also highlighted – that must be captured: date, doses, and associated symptoms or side effects.

In Figure 4.17 we also see information related to a decrease in dose that can be picked up through the operation of a fact detection.

Case Narrative
Suspect Drug: Cisplatin (CDDP)
Comed/Treatment Drugs: METHOTREXATE (METHOTREXATE) [Concomitant]
Comed/Treatment Drugs: ALLOPURINAL (ALLOPURINAL) [Concomitant]
Comed/Treatment Drugs: OMEPRAZOLE (OMEPRAZOLE) [Concomitant]
Comed/Treatment Drugs: IDARUBICIN (IDARUBICIN) [Concomitant]
Comed/Treatment Drugs: CYCLOPHOSPHAMIDE (CYCLOPHOSPHAMIDE) [Concomitant]
Comed/Treatment Drugs: Lansoprazole (Lansoprazole) [Concomitant]
Comed/Treatment Drugs: FILGRASTIM (FILGRASTIM) [Concomitant]
Comed/Treatment Drugs: VINCRISTINE (VINCRISTINE) [Concomitant]
Indication: Acute myeloid leukemia
Patient History: Current Condition : Gastritis Note:
Outcome: Complete Recovery

Inappropriate antidiuretic hormone secretion [Inappropriate antidiuretic hormone secretion]
Hyponatremia [Hyponatraemia]
Neutropenia [Neutropenia]
Ulcerative necrotic lesion [Skin ulcer]
Pseudomonas serufinose isolated in blood cultures [Pseudomonal bacterisemia]
Escherichia coli isolated in blood cultures [Escherichia bactersevia]
Aplastic marrow [Bone marrow failure]
Fever [Pyrexia]

Case History
Initial report received on 13 AUG 1999 from a physician:

This patient started treatment with Cisplatin (CDDP) 75 mb/kb 3–4 months ago for acute mylogneic
leukemia. She presented inappropriate secretion of antidiuretic hormone, due to hyponatriaemia as the
physician stated. Concomitantly she received chemotherapy.
The Cisplatin daily dose was decreased to 60 mg and excess of water intake was recommended and the
adverse event resolved. The physician considered this event as medically significant.

Follow-up information was received on 25 JUL 2000: The patient presented with dyspnea on exertion
and fatigue of 2 weeks' duration. Her past medical history was significant for gastritis for which she was
receiving Lansoprazole treatment.

A complete blood cell count demonstrated leukocytosis (white blood cells 40,000/uL), anemia
(hemoglobin 5.5 g/dL), and thrombocytopenia (platelets 100 x 100/uL).

The chemistry profile was unremarkable, apart from an elevated lactate dehydrogenase level. In the
peripheral blood smear, blasts of L1 morphology comprised 75% of the leukocytes and the bone marrow
was heavily infiltrated by blast cells that consisted of more than 85% of the marrow nucleated elements.

The patient was diagnosed with common acure lymphblastic leukemia, and treatment was initiated.
The patient received prephase treatment with intravenous prednisone 10 mg/m2 daily on days 1-5.

Figure 4.15 Typical pro-forma report output.
Source: B. deVille.

Summarization

The extracted information and post-processed information can be combined and put into a summarization task that is taken care of by SAS Content Summarization Manager.

A typical output is to prepare a case summary displayed in two or three paragraphs and sometimes displaying numerically information that would otherwise normally take many pages of textual, tabular, and graphic output.

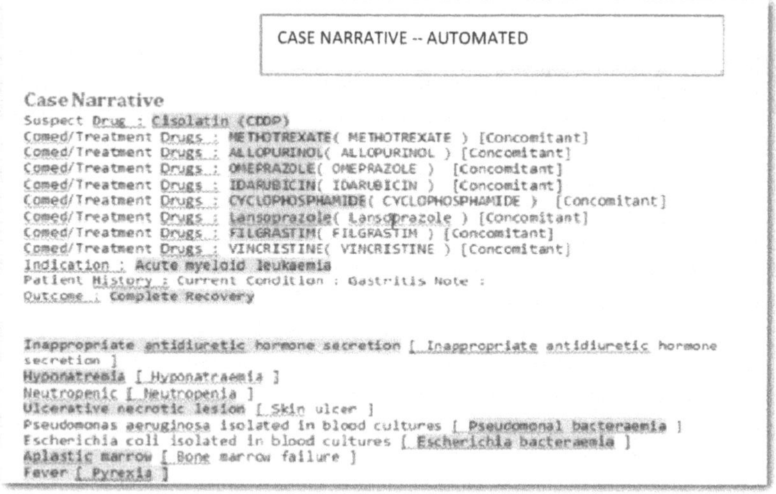

```
                    ┌─────────────────────────────────────────────┐
                    │  CASE NARRATIVE -- AUTOMATED                 │
                    └─────────────────────────────────────────────┘

  Case Narrative
  Suspect Drug : Cisplatin (CDDP)
  Comed/Treatment Drugs : METHOTREXATE( METHOTREXATE ) [Concomitant]
  Comed/Treatment Drugs : ALLOPURINOL( ALLOPURINOL ) [Concomitant]
  Comed/Treatment Drugs : OMEPRAZOLE( OMEPRAZOLE ) [Concomitant]
  Comed/Treatment Drugs : IDARUBICIN( IDARUBICIN ) [Concomitant]
  Comed/Treatment Drugs : CYCLOPHOSPHAMIDE( CYCLOPHOSPHAMIDE ) [Concomitant]
  Comed/Treatment Drugs : Lansoprazole( Lansoprazole ) [Concomitant]
  Comed/Treatment Drugs : FILGRASTIM( FILGRASTIM ) [Concomitant]
  Comed/Treatment Drugs : VINCRISTINE( VINCRISTINE ) [Concomitant]
  Indication : Acute myeloid leukaemia
  Patient History : Current Condition : Gastritis Note :
  Outcome : Complete Recovery


  Inappropriate antidiuretic hormone secretion [ Inappropriate antidiuretic hormone
  secretion ]
  Hyponatremia [ Hyponatraemia ]
  Neutropenic [ Neutropenia ]
  Ulcerative necrotic lesion [ Skin ulcer ]
  Pseudomonas aeruginosa isolated in blood cultures [ Pseudomonal bacteraemia ]
  Escherichia coli isolated in blood cultures [ Escherichia bacteraemia ]
  Aplastic marrow [ Bone marrow failure ]
  Fever [ Pyrexia ]
```

Figure 4.16 Example of raw input and recognition features.
Source: B. deVille.

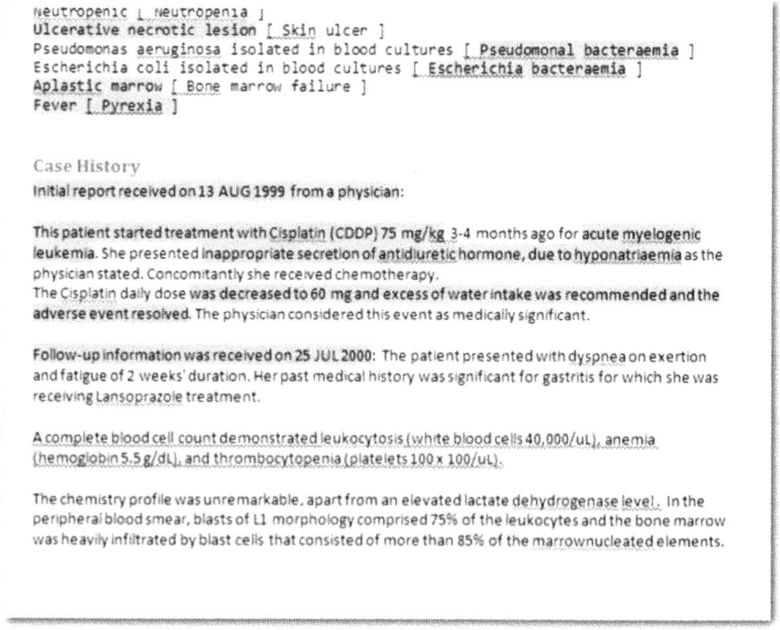

```
  Neutropenic [ Neutropenia ]
  Ulcerative necrotic lesion [ Skin ulcer ]
  Pseudomonas aeruginosa isolated in blood cultures [ Pseudomonal bacteraemia ]
  Escherichia coli isolated in blood cultures [ Escherichia bacteraemia ]
  Aplastic marrow [ Bone marrow failure ]
  Fever [ Pyrexia ]
```

Case History

Initial report received on 13 AUG 1999 from a physician:

This patient started treatment with Cisplatin (CDDP) 75 mg/kg 3-4 months ago for acute myelogenic leukemia. She presented inappropriate secretion of antidiuretic hormone, due to hyponatriaemia as the physician stated. Concomitantly she received chemotherapy.
The Cisplatin daily dose was decreased to 60 mg and excess of water intake was recommended and the adverse event resolved. The physician considered this event as medically significant.

Follow-up information was received on 25 JUL 2000: The patient presented with dyspnea on exertion and fatigue of 2 weeks' duration. Her past medical history was significant for gastritis for which she was receiving Lansoprazole treatment.

A complete blood cell count demonstrated leukocytosis (white blood cells 40,000/uL), anemia (hemoglobin 5.5 g/dL), and thrombocytopenia (platelets 100 x 100/uL).

The chemistry profile was unremarkable, apart from an elevated lactate dehydrogenase level. In the peripheral blood smear, blasts of L1 morphology comprised 75% of the leukocytes and the bone marrow was heavily infiltrated by blast cells that consisted of more than 85% of the marrow nucleated elements.

Figure 4.17 Results of conditional inference.
Source: B. deVille.

Once information is captured as a data table, it can be postprocessed so that, in this case shown earlier, we can add up the number of chemotherapy instances that have been identified. This can be used to generate a textual description that takes the number of summed chemotherapy instances as one of its inputs. The date range can also be collected, and this too can be echoed in the textual description that is produced.

The extracted information and the post processed information can be combined and can be put into a summarization task that can be used to produce a pro forma summary of the information that has been captured for presentation. An example of this is shown in Figure 4.18.

Source record	Pro forma Summary
Diagnosis of metastatic ovarian cancer 7/19	Diagnosis of metastatic ovarian cancer 7/19.
Diagnosis of benign hypertension 7/28	
Multiple treatments of surgery 8/2 and chemotherapy 8/16 – 1/17	Multiple treatment of surgery 8/2 and chemotherapy 8/16 – 1/7.
Patient readmitted 7/24	
Treatment of intravenous medications (4 times) dates 12/24 – 1//06 duration: 12 days	Treatment of intravenous medications (4 times) dates 12/24 – 1/06. Duration 12 days.
Treatment of chemotherapy (7 times) Dates mm/yy – 01/02 duration: 14 months.	
Treament of abdominal catheter placement date 01/02.	Treatment of chemotherapy (7 times) dates xx/yy – 01/02. Duration 14 months.
Referred for management of inpatient admission	
Medical Director note: cancer of ovary mets to liver. Peritonitis, ascites, abd pain. Date 12/23	Released for management of inpatient admission.
Medical Director note: cancer of ovary mets to liver. Peritonitis, ascites, abd pain. Date 01/02	Medical Director note. Cancer of ovary metx to liver. Peritonitis, ancites, abd pain. Date 12/23.
Discharged to inpatient hospice date 1/10	
Admission – discharge: 19 days	Discharged to inpatient hospice date 1/10.
	Admission – discharge: 19 days

Figure 4.18 Source-target production of the pro forma summary.
Source: B. deVille.

Diagnosis of metastatic ovarian cancer 7/19.|

Multiple treatment of surgery 8/2 and chemotherapy 8/16 – 1/7.

Patient readmitted 7/24.

Treatment of intravenous medications (4 times) dates 12/24 – 1/06. Duration 12 days.

Treatment of chemotherapy (7 times) dates xx/yy – 01/02. Duration 14 months.

Released for management of inpatient admission.

Medical Director note. Cancer of ovary metx to liver. Peritonitis, ancites, abd pain. Date 12/23.

Discharged to inpatient hospice date 1/10.

Admission – discharge: 19 days

Figure 4.19 Pro forma summary.
Source: B. deVille.

Finally, the pro forma summary can be edited in a document editor to produce a final review version of the desired presentation document. An example end product is shown in Figure 4.19.

CONCLUSION

Here we have demonstrated six basic operations that provide a blend of linguistic and quantitative text analytic processing – together with associated report production capabilities that are suitable for the construction of an automated report production process in the preparation of PSUR reports.

These operations are:

- Categorization
- Conceptual extraction
- Event-object detection and quantitative summarization/ arithmetic
- Conditional inference
- Fact extraction
- Sentiment extraction

Our business analysis has demonstrated significant economies in the deployment of such a system. Alternative workflows can be set up to ensure various layers of human review. There are significant benefits in the development of a central repository of documents. Even greater economies – difficult to quantify – are delivered by virtue of the important quality control function that is provided by computation.

NOTES

i. F. Mosteller and D.L. Wallace., *Inference and Disputed Authorship: The Federalist* (Reading, MA: Addison-Wesley, 1964).

ii. G. Fung, "The Disputed *Federalist Papers*: SVM Feature Selection via Concave Minimization," *Proceedings of the 2003 Conference on Diversity in Computing* (ACM Press, 2003), 42–46.

iii. J.W. Pennebaker, *The Secret Life of Pronouns* (Bloomsbury, NY: Bloomsbury Press, 2011).

iv. M. Koppel, J. Schler, and S. Argamon, "Computational Methods in Authorship Attribution," *Journal of the American Society for Information Science and Technology* 60 (1) (2009): 9–26. https://doi.org/10.1002/asi.20961.

v. M.A.K. Halliday and C.M.I.M. Matthiessen, *An Introduction to Functional Grammar* (London: Hodder Arnold, 2003).

vi. Google. (2010). n-gram viewer https://en.wikipedia.org/wiki/Google_Ngram_Viewer.

vii. J.W. Pennebaker, R.J. Booth, and M.E. Francis, *Linguistic Inquiry and Word Count (LIWC2007): A text analysis program* (Austin, TX: Pennebaker Conglomerates, Inc., 2007). www.LIWC.net.

viii. J.W. Pennebaker, *The Secret Life of Pronouns* (Bloomsbury, NY: Bloomsbury Press, 2011).

ix. J.W. Pennebaker and L.A. King, "Linguistic styles: Language use as an individual difference," *Journal of Personality and Social Psychology* 77 (1999): 1296–1312.

x. M.L. Newman, C.J. Groom, L.D. Handelman, and J.W. Pennebaker, "Gender Differences in Language Use: An Analysis of 14,000 Text Samples," *Discourse Processes* 45 (2008): 211–246.

xi. J.W. Pennebaker and L.D. Stone, "Words of Wisdom: Language Use Over the Life Span," *Journal of Personality and Social Psychology* 85 (2) (2002): 291–301.

xii. K. Peng and R.E. Nisbett, "Culture, Dialectics, and Reasoning about Contradiction," *American Psychologist* 54 (9) (Sept. 1999): 741–754.

xiii. C.K. Chung and J.W. Pennebaker, "The Psychological Function of Function Words," *Social Communication: Frontiers of Social Psychology* (ed. K. Fiedler), (New York: Psychology Press, 2007). 343–359.

xiv. B. deVille and M. Wolff, *Error Reduction and Report Automation Approaches for Textually Dense. Pharmaceutical Regulatory Conformance Incident Data.* SAS Global Forum, Paper 180-2012 (Cary, NC: SAS Institute Inc., 2012), https://support.sas.com/resources /papers/proceedings12/180-2012.pdf.

xv. SAS Institute Inc., *SAS® Visual Text Analytics 8.3: User's Guide* (Cary, NC: SAS Institute Inc., 2018).

xvi. VAERS. https://vaers.hhs.gov/about.html (accessed, June 1, 2020).

xvii. For more information on Perl Regular Expressions, see J.E.F. Friedl, *Mastering Regular Expressions*, third edition (Sebastopol, CA: O'Reilly Media Inc., 2006).

xviii. José Ferreirós, "The Road to Modern Logic—An Interpretation," *Bulletin of Symbolic Logic*, 7 (4) (2001); 2001, pp. 441–484, doi:10.2307/2687794, JSTOR 2687794.

CHAPTER 5

Textual Abstraction: Latent Structure, Dimension Reduction

TEXT MINING DATA SOURCE ASSEMBLY

One of the lively areas in text analytics is the area of topic modeling. This includes topic modeling techniques like latent semantic analysis (LSA)[i], latent Dirichlet allocation (LDA) as popularized by Blei,[ii] and the SAS approach to text topics described by Cox.[iii] These approaches employ a variety of statistical techniques to detect the underlying dimensionality in collections of textual data in order to infer the common topical content that is driving the observed behavior of the text.

LATENT STRUCTURE AND DIMENSIONAL REDUCTION

A classic discussion of using linear products to compress collections of text documents encoded as matrix representations is given by Albright[iv]. The collection can be expressed as a word x document representation that can be manipulated and summarized using a range of matrix manipulation approaches, drawn from *linear algebra*. The approach that employs singular value decomposition is discussed here.

To set the stage, Albright used a set of documents collected from various diagnostics issued by the SAS processor. Each message is treated as a separate document:

- Error: Invalid message file format
- Error: Unable to open message file using message path
- Error: Unable to format variable

The way the terms and documents are represented to facilitate computation is as a term by document matrix. This is shown in Table 5.1.

Table 5.1 Example Term by Document Table

Term Number	1	2	3	4	5	6	7	8	9	10	11
	error	invalid	message	file	format	unable	to	open	using	path	variable
doc 1	1	1	1	1	1	0	0	0	0	0	0
doc 2	1	0	2	1	0	1	1	1	1	1	0
doc 3	1	0	0	0	1	1	1	0	0	0	1

Table 5.2 Example Term-Document Co-occurrence Table

Term number		Cross-Product	
1	error	d1 × d2	d1 × d3
2	invalid	1 . 1	1 . 1
3	message		
4	file	1 . 2	
5	format	1 . 1	
6	unable		1 . 1
7	to		
8	open		
9	using		
10	path		
11	variable		
	Total	**4**	**2**

To illustrate an algorithmic way of detecting similarities between documents, we can take the cross-products of term co-occurrence in a pairwise fashion as shown in Table 5.2.

Using this technique, we can see that documents 1 and 2 are more similar than documents 1 and 3. We can use linear algebra to formalize and extend this approach in a considerably scaled up way and this becomes a major piece of the text-to-data engine used in text analytics.

Singular Value Decomposition as Dimension Reduction

Let's see how singular value decomposition can be used to surface semantic structure using our simple example here. We begin by defining the term-document representation as matrix **A**. This is a $m \times n$ term-document frequency matrix that has m terms and n documents so that there are more terms than documents: $m \geq n$. Matrix **A** is always more or less *sparse;* that is, when we look at the matrix, there are more gaps in the entries than numbers. This is true throughout most text analytics applications.

With this kind of representation, it is possible to use linear algebra to recombine the rows and columns of the matrix so as to arrange denser combinations of terms along vertical columns that are collected together according to mathematical "stickiness" that is created by forming a linear equation that collects the terms together. One of the primary mechanisms for this is singular value decomposition.

The singular value decomposition of **A** can be stated as follows (here k ≤ n):

$$\mathbf{A} = \mathbf{U}\boldsymbol{\Sigma}\mathbf{V}^k$$

where **U** is an $n \times k$ regular matrix with columns that make up the left singular vectors, **Σ** is an $k \times k$ dimensional diagonal matrix whose diagonal elements are termed singular values, and **V** is an $k \times m$ transpose matrix whose columns form the right singular vectors of **A**. The entire relationship preserves the original values of **A** yet rearranges them so that the sparseness of **A** is pushed into denser expressions that can economically capture the co-occurrence relationships among the terms in the document collection. This general process is often referred to as latent semantic analysis.

A schematic representation of this process is illustrated in Figure 5.1.

As shown in Figure 5.2, the key products from this rearrangement are the **U** weights, which can be applied against the original **A** matrix to create the SVD dimensional products for the three original documents (shown in Figure 5.2 as SVD1 and SVD2).

In this illustration, we have shown how the terms have been compressed into two dimensions. These two new dimensions are used

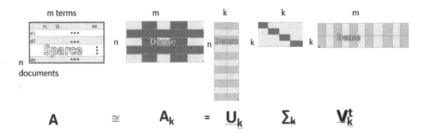

Figure 5.1 The factorization process.
Source: B. deVille.

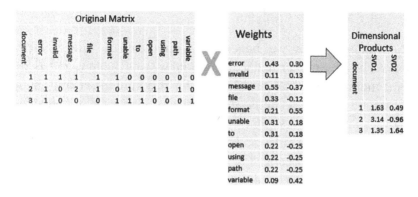

Figure 5.2 SVDs for a term-document frequency matrix.
Source: B. deVille.

to create two new variables, SVD1 and SVD2, naming conventions for "singular value dimension 1" and "singular value dimension 2," respectively. These two new fields represent dimensional reduction and feature extraction – reducing a larger number of fields of information into a smaller, more manageable number of fields. At this point, we could say that in this example, we now have two fields to represent the contents of the original documents that consist of 11 terms. The two fields are SVD constructs where the field value for the feature is a dimensional score that sums the U-weights for each of the 11 included terms in each of the documents. The dimensional products are formed by the matrix multiplication between the original matrix and the weights. This approach is aligned with a number of dimensional reduction approaches that include principal component analysis, factor analysis, and discriminant analysis.

At the moment, the SVD scores themselves are simply numeric representations. We can get a sense of how the dimensions capture the term values and meaning by looking at the weight loadings of the terms on the dimensions. The weight loadings are shown in the "Weights" table in Figure 5.2. We can see that the first SVD has a 0.43 weight on "error" and a 0.55 weight on "message." The second SVD has a 0.55 weight on "format," 0.42 weight on "variable," and a 0.30 weight on "error." We could say that both dimensions display an association with *errors*. The emphasis of the first SVD is on error *messages* and the second SVD seems to emphasize *format* errors.

Latent Semantic Analysis

The examples that we have been using employ linear algebra approaches to summarize documents and so as to pull out underlying semantic meaning. The generic term for this kind of semantic summarization is latent semantic analysis (LSA). Albright et al.[v] provide a slightly more robust example using a data set that was extracted from Reuters newswire stories and that had been preassigned categories based on manual tagging. The advantage of this data set is that it is possible to carry out a latent semantic analysis with the goal of identifying these manual, preassigned semantic categories. If we can do this algorithmically, then we can show the value of automated approaches to text description and summarization.

The example data extracted from Albright et al. is shown in Table 5.3. The data and associated analysis are also reproduced in the SAS Institute[vi] text analytics reference manual. The example demonstrates how LSA can be used to automatically uncover the preassigned manually tagged categories of the documents.

Now render the documents in the form of a term x document matrix (see Table 5.4).

Table 5.3 Example Newswire-like text to Illustrate LSA

Document	Text	Category
1	deposit the cash and check in the bank	finance
2	the river boat is on the bank	river
3	borrow based on credit	finance
4	river boat floats up the river	river
5	boat is by the dock near the bank	river
6	with credit, I can borrow cash from the bank	finance
7	boat floats by dock near the river bank	river
8	check the parade route to see the floats	parade
9	along the parade route	parade

Source: Adapted from Albright, R., Cox, J., and Daly, K. (2001). *Skinning the Cat: Comparing Alternative Text Mining Algorithms for Categorization.* Proceedings of the 2nd Data Mining Conference of DiaMondSUG, DM Paper 113. Chicago, IL.

Table 5.4 Term *x* Document Matrix Representation for Newswire Data

	The	cash	check	bank	river	boat	+ be	on	borrow	credit	+ floats	by	dock	near	parade	route
d1	2	1	1	1	0	0	0	0	0	0	0	0	0	0	0	0
d2	2	0	0	1	1	1	1	1	0	0	0	0	0	0	0	0
d3	0	0	0	0	0	0	0	1	1	1	0	0	0	0	0	0
d4	1	0	0	0	2	1	0	0	0	0	1	0	0	0	0	0
d5	2	0	0	1	0	1	1	0	0	0	0	1	1	1	0	0
d6	1	1	0	1	0	0	0	0	1	1	0	0	0	0	0	0
d7	1	0	0	1	1	1	0	0	0	0	1	1	1	1	0	0
d8	2	0	1	0	0	0	0	0	0	0	1	0	0	0	1	1
d9	1	0	0	0	0	0	0	0	0	0	0	0	0	0	1	1

Clustering Approach to Document Classification

As a step to calculating the co-occurrence of terms between documents, compute a binary absence-presence metric for each term in all the documents (see Table 5.5).

Table 5.5 Binary Co-Occurrence Matrix for Newswire Data

	The	cash	check	bank	river	boat	+ be	on	borrow	credit	+ floats	by	dock	near	parade	route
d1	1	1	1	1	0	0	0	0	0	0	0	0	0	0	0	0
d2	1	0	0	1	1	1	1	1	0	0	0	0	0	0	0	0
d3	0	0	0	0	0	0	0	1	1	1	0	0	0	0	0	0
d4	1	0	0	0	1	1	0	0	0	0	1	0	0	0	0	0
d5	1	0	0	1	0	1	1	0	0	0	0	1	1	1	0	0
d6	1	1	0	1	0	0	0	0	1	1	0	0	0	0	0	0
d7	1	0	0	1	1	1	0	0	0	0	1	1	1	1	0	0
d8	1	0	1	0	0	0	0	0	0	0	1	0	0	0	1	1
d9	1	0	0	0	0	0	0	0	0	0	0	0	0	0	1	1

If we take the binary co-occurrence and cluster on term similarity, we get a result shown in Table 5.6.

In Table 5.6 we see that Cluster 1 (consisting of documents d1–d6) has strong term associations across the first 12 terms in the data set. Cluster 2 is further broken down into two subclusters – one associated with the terms "bank," "boat," "by," "dock," "near," and the other associated with the terms "parade" and "route."

Table 5.6 Clustering Term-Documents by Term Co-Occurrence

Cluster 1	The	cash	check	bank	river	boat	+ be	on	borrow	credit	+ floats	by	dock	near	parade	route
d1	1	1	1	1	0	0	0	0	0	0	0	0	0	0	0	0
d2	1	0	0	1	1	1	1	1	0	0	0	0	0	0	0	0
d3	0	0	0	0	0	0	0	1	1	1	0	0	0	0	0	0
d4	1	0	0	0	1	1	0	0	0	0	1	0	0	0	0	0
d6	1	1	0	1	0	0	0	0	1	1	0	0	0	0	0	0
	-	-	-	-	-	-	-	-	-	-	-	-	o	o	o	o
Cluster 2																
d5	1	0	0	1	0	1	1	0	0	0	0	1	1	1	0	0
d7	1	0	0	1	1	1	0	0	0	0	1	1	1	1	0	0
d8	1	0	1	0	0	0	0	0	0	0	1	0	0	0	1	1
d9	1	0	0	0	0	0	0	0	0	0	0	0	0	0	1	1
		x						x	x	x		x	x	x		x
Cluster 2.1																
d5	1	0	0	1	0	1	1	0	0	0	0	1	1	1	0	0
d7	1	0	0	1	1	1	0	0	0	0	1	1	1	1	0	0
			x	x	x	x						x	x			
Cluster 2.2																
d8	1	0	1	0	0	0	0	0	0	0	1	0	0	0	1	1
d9	1	0	0	0	0	0	0	0	0	0	0	0	0	0	1	1
			x												x	x

If we look at the original categories, shown in Table 5.3, we see that clustering on term co-occurrence only does an approximate job of classifying the original set of documents into the appropriate categories. This example shows the advantages of using clustering approaches to summarize semantic content in documents but also suggests some of the disadvantages. Our interest in doing a better job at classifying the documents into their original categories motivates us to explore the potential of latent semantic indexing using the SVD approach.

SVD Approach to Document Indexing

We begin by computing singular value products (using the equation of $\mathbf{A} = \mathbf{U\Sigma V}^k$) and displaying SVD products by term as shown in Table 5.7.

Table 5.7 Singular Value Weights for Newswire Terms – Three Dimensions

	SV1	SV2	SV3
along	−0.01	0.00	0.20
bank	−0.46	0.47	−0.10
based	0.00	0.07	−0.01
boat	−0.49	−0.16	−0.14
borrow	−0.05	0.34	−0.03
can	−0.05	0.27	−0.02
cash	−0.10	0.47	0.04
check	−0.08	0.19	0.39
credit	0.00	0.07	−0.01
credit,	−0.05	0.27	−0.02
deposit	−0.05	0.20	0.06
dock	−0.26	0.02	−0.10
floats	−0.33	−0.21	0.31
near	−0.26	0.02	−0.10
parade	−0.04	−0.01	0.52
river	−0.52	−0.38	−0.06
route	−0.04	−0.01	0.52
see	−0.04	−0.01	0.33

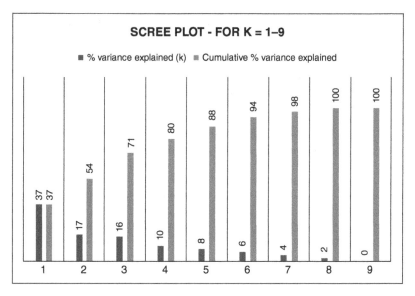

Figure 5.3 Text variance explained by singular value dimensional products for values of *k*.
Source: B. deVille.

Figure 5.3 displays a scree plot of the variance explained by the singular value products for *k* = 1–9. There is no general method of selecting the *k* best singular value dimensions and there is usually a trade-off between interpretability and comprehensiveness. The scree plot is a useful tool in visually identifying good values for *k*. In our case, we can see a sharp fall-off of variance explained with three SVD dimensional products, so we set this as our cutoff of selected dimensions.

ROUGH MEANING – APPROXIMATION FOR SINGULAR VALUE DIMENSIONS

As a preliminary step to establishing a sense of the semantic meaning of the three singular value dimensional products that we have selected, it is useful to see which terms are closely associated with the dimensional product. We can establish this association by looking at the strength or size of the associated coefficients shown in Table 5.7. At this point we are mainly concerned with strength and will ignore whether the coefficient is positive or negative. We will see later in the computation of topics we fine tune the dimensional products by rotating their orientation in cartesian space to manipulate the association between terms and dimensions and also minimize the impact of positive and negative coefficients. At this point, let's just identify high-weighted terms for each of the three SVD dimensions. This yields the following:

- The highest-weighted terms on SVD1 are "river" (–0.52), "bank" (–0.45), "boat" (–0.49), and "dock" (–0.26), all river-related nautical terms. Let's call this the "river" SVD.
- The highest-weighted terms on SVD2 are "borrow," "cash," "credit," "deposit," "floats," and "river," predominantly financial terms. Let's call this the "finance" SVD.
- The highest-weighted terms on SVD3 are "check," "floats," "parade," "route," and "see" parade-associated terms. Let's call this the "parade" SVD.

Our next step is to compute the SVD score on each SVD composite vector for each document. This means that each document will carry a score that shows its affinity for the "river" SVD, the "finance" SVD, and the "parade" SVD.

Semantic Indexing: Assigning Category Based on Singular Value Dimensional Scores

Latent semantic indexing is the process of establishing semantic content for a document based on its association with dimensional products, such as the singular value dimensions illustrated here. The first step of this process is to compute the weighted association between the terms in the document and the dimensional product value for that document. The results of this calculation are shown in Table 5.8.

For ease of interpretation, express the SVD product scores for each document in absolute terms (making all the numbers positive). These results are shown in Table 5.9.

Here we see that documents 2, 4, 5, and 7 are clustered together with the highest score on the "river" SVD.

Table 5.8 Singular Value Dimensional Scores for Each Document Based on All Weighted Term Values Summed over the Dimension

Document	SV1 "river"	SV2 "finance"	SV3 "parade"
1	−0.18	0.51	0.16
2	−0.39	−0.02	−0.12
3	−0.02	0.19	−0.01
4	−0.49	−0.43	0.02
5	−0.39	0.13	−0.17
6	−0.19	0.70	−0.05
7	−0.61	−0.09	−0.07
8	−0.14	−0.02	0.82
9	−0.02	−0.01	0.50

Table 5.9 Absolute Singular Value Dimensional Scores for Each Document

Document	Absolute SV1	Absolute SV2	Absolute SV3
1	0.18	**0.51**	0.16
2	**0.39**	0.02	0.12
3	0.02	**0.19**	0.01
4	**0.49**	0.43	0.02
5	**0.39**	0.13	0.17
6	0.19	**0.70**	0.05
7	**0.61**	0.09	0.07
8	0.14	0.02	**0.82**
9	0.02	0.01	**0.50**

Documents 1, 3, and 6 are clustered together with the highest score on the "financial" SVD, and documents 8 and 9 are clustered together with the highest score on the "parade" SVD.

If we compare these results with the manually tagged categories of the newswire articles outlined at the beginning of the section we can see there is a full correspondence between the manually tagged categories and the SVD-derived categories. This is an example of how an automated approach can be used to duplicate the results of a more manually intense process. It also provides an example of how

Table 5.10 Performance of Cluster Derived and SVD Derived Semantic
Categories

	Manual Category	Cluster Categories	SVD Categories
d1	finance	1	1
d2	river	1	2
d3	finance	1	1
d4	river	1	2
d5	river	3	2
d6	finance	1	1
d7	river	3	2
d8	parade	2	3
d9	parade	2	3

SVD-derived semantic products perform better than semantic summaries produced by cluster analysis. These results are displayed in Table 5.10.

Identifying Topics Using Latent Structure

In the example above the authors demonstrated that singular value composites could provide an accurate method to automatically identify semantic content in collections of documents. In this case, the latent semantic indexing approach correctly identified all of the manually assigned categories in the newswire snippets. When this approach is generalized, it becomes a reliable and flexible method to identify the topical content of a wide range of documents and, as discussed in Cox,[vii] serves as a generally superior alternative to the usual approach of identifying topics through the latent Dirichlet allocation (LDA) method.[viii]

The SAS approach to topics is aligned with the well-established practice of factor analysis that has stood the test of time in a range of data analytic tasks; for example, a similar approach is used to summarize and extract a wide range of data management, dimensional reduction tasks used in deriving such psychometric measures as the Myers-Briggs score.[ix] SAS topics complement typical hierarchical clustering approaches where each document is mapped to a unique culture: since each document can be scored on its affinity to a range of topics, this means that any given document can be assigned to multiple topics at varying levels of strengths.

SAS topics are computed by employing a factor analytic approach of factor rotation in order to find the best alignment of terms to the underlying dimensions. SAS can do either a Varimax for orthogonal rotation or Promax for nonorthogonal rotation. The main effect of the rotation is to maximize the sum of the squared weights on each individual term; this has the effect of isolating a set of terms with large weight in absolute value and to have most other term weights fall closer to zero. The approach has a number of benefits in producing unambiguous semantic meanings for the term-dimension associations. Both orthogonal (uncorrelated) and oblique (correlated) topic rotations are supported by SAS topics.

The effect of factor rotation is illustrated in Figure 5.4. Here we show the term weights plotted between two sets of words in the document collection with two lines projected for the original singular value decomposition (SVD) and the associated rotated SVD line. The top of the diagram illustrates the drop of the weight from original SVD value to the rotated SVD value.

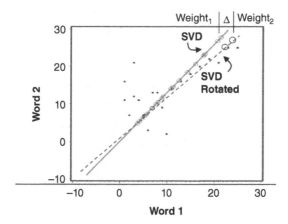

Figure 5.4 Illustration of effect of rotation in the SVD projections in a collection of documents (here showing two word term weights plotted against one another).
Source: Adapted from R. Albright, *Taming Text with the SVD* (Cary, NC: SAS Institute Inc., 2004).

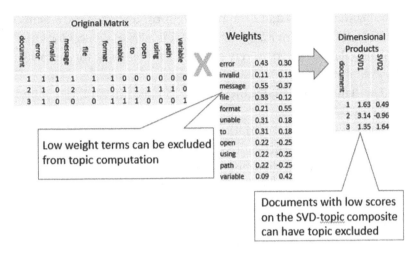

Figure 5.5 Example of adjustments to SVD computation in the construction of topics: term thresholds and document SVD score thresholds.
Source: B. deVille.

As shown in Figure 5.5, more user control in the derivation of the topic is provided by allowing the user to specify a cutoff value for the identification of a term coefficient loading on the associated semantic dimension. Finally, a document-level cutoff is offered so that a given topic in a document is only presented for robust document-topic scores. These user-adjustable steps are important interventions in the identification of meaningful semantic dimensions for the topics. They also speed the computation of these derived text indicators when it comes time to score the documents for processing.

Latent Structure: Tracking Topic Term Variability Across Semantic Fields

Leskovec, Backstrom, and Kleinberg[x] demonstrate an algorithmic approach to identifying and clustering textual variants of news quotes to track news topics over time (even as meanings and interpretations of specific vocabularies change in different contexts and time periods). The approach is useful in recognizing that, while specific words and terms may change somewhat in different contexts, they nevertheless indicate a common theme. To illustrate the approach to differentiating topical content in textual data in different contexts, we use a publicly available data set from Kaggle that contains a list of descriptions of the most popular Kaggle data sets sorted on the basis of the number of votes obtained.[xi]

The data set illustrated here has 2150 records and 15 columns, shown in Table 5.11.

The last column – Description – is the field of interest for our analysis. The description entries are treated as the documents under study.

Figure 5.6 gives a snapshot of the data.

Once the data has been loaded into the environment, we apply the preprocessing steps and then fit the SVD topic model.

Once the model is fitted, each document is weighted with respect to each of the fitted topics. These weights for each document–topic combination signify how each topic is represented in the documents. Every document gets represented as a combination of all of the topics with some weights (in our application, we have considered 15). For each document, the topic with highest weight is tagged – or associated – with that document.

Table 5.12 shows the distribution of estimates for each document across all of the topics.

In Table 5.12, we observe the weights for the first two documents of the data set for each topic. For the first document, topic 11 has the highest weight. For the second document, topic 14 has the highest. We tag each document with the topic with the highest estimate.

Table 5.11 Columns in the Voted Kaggle Data Set

Kaggle "Voted" Data Columns	
Title	License
Subtitle	Views
Owner	Downloads
Vote	Kernels
Version History	Topics
Tags	URL
Datatype	Description
Size	

id	Title	Subtitle	Owner	Votes
1	Credit Card Fraud Detection	Anonymized credit card transactions labeled as frau...	Machine Learning Group - ULB	1241
2	European Soccer Database	25k+ matches, players & teams attributes for Europe ...	Hugo Mathien	1046
3	TMDB 5000 Movie Dataset	Metadata on ~5,000 movies from TMDb	The Movie Database (TMDb)	1024
4	Global Terrorism Database	More than 170,000 terrorist attacks worldwide, 1970-...	START Consortium	789
5	Bitcoin Historical Data	Bitcoin data at 1-min intervals from select exchanges...	Zielak	618
6	Kaggle ML and Data Science Survey, 2017	A big picture view of the state of data science and m ...	Kaggle	574
7	Iris Species	Classify iris plants into three species in this classic d...	UCI Machine Learning	512
8	World Development Indicators	Explore country development indicators from around...	World Bank	468
9	Daily News for Stock Market Prediction	Using 8 years daily news headlines to predict stock ...	Aaron7sun	438
10	Pokemon with stats	721 Pokemon with stats and types	Alberto Barradas	428
11	Lending Club Loan Data	Analyze Lending Club's issued loans	Wendy Kan	406
12	Wine Reviews	130k wine reviews with variety, location, winery, pri...	zackthoutt	397

Figure 5.6 Snapshot of Kaggle test data.
Source: G. Singh Bawa

Table 5.12 Document Topic Weights

Document	Topic	Weights
1	1	0.000163
1	2	0.000163
1	3	0.000163
1	4	0.000163
1	5	0.000163
1	6	0.000163
1	7	0.000163
1	8	0.000163
1	9	0.000163
1	10	0.000163
1	11	0.997711
1	12	0.000163
1	13	0.000163
1	14	0.000163
1	15	0.000163

Document	Topic	Weights
2	1	0.000084
2	2	0.000084
2	3	0.000084
2	4	0.000084
2	5	0.000084
2	6	0.000084
2	7	0.000084
2	8	0.000084
2	9	0.000084
2	10	0.000084
2	11	0.000084
2	12	0.000084
2	13	0.000084
2	14	0.998826
2	15	0.000084

The distribution of topics across all documents under study is shown in Table 5.13.

Each topic can be represented as a combination of all the words in the corpus. Within each topic, some words have a higher topic-word weight. This implies that the words having higher weights as given by the SVD weighting contribute more for that particular topic and thereby have more semantic relevance.

The first three topics computed with the top 20 words for each, are illustrated in Table 5.14.

Now, since our topic of interest is topic 3, we create a binary target variable with all documents tagged to topic 3 as 1 and remaining as 0. This gives us 96 documents, which contain topic 3, yielding a target event rate of approximately 4 percent.

To explore topic term variability in different contexts, we create two subsets in the data set using self-organizing maps (SOMs). Since SOMs create homogenous clusters, we do this to ensure that the two resulting subcommunities have some distinguishing

Table 5.13 Topic Distribution across Documents

Topic	Count of Documents
1	92
2	138
3	96
4	266
5	111
6	123
7	127
8	181
9	155
10	124
11	89
12	171
13	137
14	160
15	175

characteristics that identify them and that distinguish them from the other subset.

After obtaining subsets, we check the event rate in the subsets to make sure that the event rate distribution of both the subsets are similar. Now, we establish the relative importance of top characteristic tokens for topic 3 when modeled separately on the subsets, to show how the tokens are impacting documents tagged as topic 3.

We use a neural network setup where the input X variables are the corresponding TF-IDF measures of each token against every document for the respective subset corpus. For the target Y variable, we use the binary target values where 1 represents the presence of topic 3.

The top 30 terms with highest weights from topic 3 are used as the feature vector. Table 5.15 shows the 30 terms with the highest weights taken from topic 3.

We use the "neuralnet" package to fit the model (https://www.rdocumentation.org/packages/neuralnet/versions/1.44.2/topics/neuralnet).

Table 5.14 Top Twenty Word Distributions by Topic

Topic	Term	Beta
1	Job	0.006949
1	Fire	0.006261
1	Years	0.005818
1	Percent	0.00502
1	Float	0.004875
1	Total	0.004792
1	Cancer	0.004658
1	Age	0.004353
1	Rate	0.003914
1	Salary	0.003903
1	Code	0.003583
1	Collection	0.003468
1	Unit	0.003231
1	Museum	0.003193
1	Daca	0.003125
1	Federal	0.0031
1	Year	0.003049
1	Employees	0.002957
1	Based	0.002943
1	Frequency	0.002892

Topic	Term	Beta
2	state	0.006336
2	year	0.005372
2	air	0.005329
2	national	0.005303
2	quality	0.004995
2	database	0.004511
2	code	0.004487
2	energy	0.004295
2	event	0.003749
2	solar	0.003452
2	states	0.003406
2	years	0.003309
2	united	0.00325
2	health	0.003145
2	public	0.003144
2	species	0.003072
2	monitoring	0.003046
2	location	0.003045
2	county	0.003042
2	system	0.003039

Topic	Term	Beta
3	model	0.016699
3	numeric	0.012199
3	features	0.011811
3	pretrained	0.011649
3	Text	0.009903
3	trained	0.007648
3	models	0.005701
3	networks	0.005664
3	Word	0.005511
3	learning	0.005231
3	deep	0.004764
3	depth	0.004762
3	vectors	0.004628
3	residual	0.004507
3	learned	0.00439
3	transferable	0.004022
3	recognition	0.003769
3	imagenet	0.003744
3	authors	0.003539
3	representations	0.003521

Table 5.15 Features for the Neural Network Setup

model	models	vectors	authors	layers
numeric	networks	residual	representations	learn
features	word	learned convolutional	images	images
pretrained	learning	transferable	child	network
text	deep	recognition	collection	lot
trained	depth	imagenet	accuracy	image

In the neural network setup, the feature vectors need to be normalized prior to model fitting. Hence, we build a scale function that employs a normalization using mean and standard deviation of the variables.

For demonstration of the application, we choose one hidden layer with 20 nodes in a setup, approximately 2100 data points, 30 input nodes, and 1 output node. The activation function used is sigmoid (logistic in the package) and the remaining arguments have been kept as the original default settings. The arguments in the neural network are shown in Table 5.16.

Table 5.16 Arguments for Neural Network Function

Argument	Value Used
Formula	~ accuracy + authors + child + collection + convolutional + deep + depth + features + image + imagenet + images + layers + learn + learned + learning +lot + model + models + network + networks + numeric + pretrained + recognition + representations + residual + text + trained + transferable + vectors + word
Data	First, the TFIDF data is scaled to normalize using z-transformation.
Number of hidden layers	1, to remove complexity
Number of hidden nodes	20 for simplicity
Activation Function used	Sigmoid or "logistic"

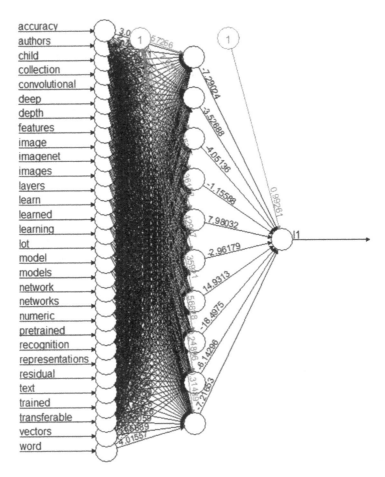

Figure 5.7 Plot of fitted neural network on the entire dataset (screen shot).
Source: G. Singh Bawa.

A diagram of the fitted neural network model is shown in Figure 5.7.

Once the model is fitted, we observe the relative importance of each of the features. These features are shown in Figure 5.8.

The 30 input tokens, when arranged in order of their relative importance in explaining the variability of topic 3, are shown

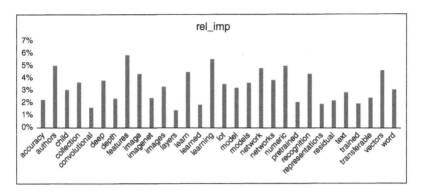

Figure 5.8 Relative importance for each of the explanatory variables (subset 1). *Source:* G. Singh Bawa.

in Table 5.17. The table shows a substantial number of tokens out of the top 20 terms from topic 3. The highlighted tokens are the ones that were present earlier in the top 20 word-topic distribution of topic 3.

It can be noted that the top 20 terms from the neural network output that were not present in the SVD output have a combined relative importance of about 28 percent compared to the roughly 14 percent combined importance of the highlighted terms, which missed out in the SVD setup. The new terms explain around 14 percent more variability.

Now, in order to show the importance of subsets, we implement a similar neural network model on the two subsets. All of the setup remains the same except for the number of input documents, which has become half of the initial setup; thus, the number of hidden nodes now used is 10 instead of 20.

The neural network plots for the two subsets are shown in Figures 5.9 and 5.10.

We observe the relative importance of the terms from subset 1 neural network. Since both the subsets are similar in terms of event distribution, relative importance and rank ordering of terms are

Table 5.17 Relative Importance of Terms

Terms	Relative Importance	Rank from SVD
Features	6%	3
Learning	6%	10
Numeric	5%	2
Authors	5%	19
Network	5%	
Vectors	5%	13
Learn	5%	
Recognition	4%	17
Image	4%	
Networks	4%	8
Deep	4%	11
Collection	4%	
Models	4%	7
Lot	4%	
Images	3%	
Model	3%	1
Word	3%	9
Child	3%	
Text	3%	5
Transferable	2%	16
Imagenet	2%	18
Depth	2%	12
Accuracy	2%	
Residual	2%	14
Pretrained	2%	4
Trained	2%	6
representations	2%	20
Learned	2%	15
convolutional	2%	
Layers	1%	

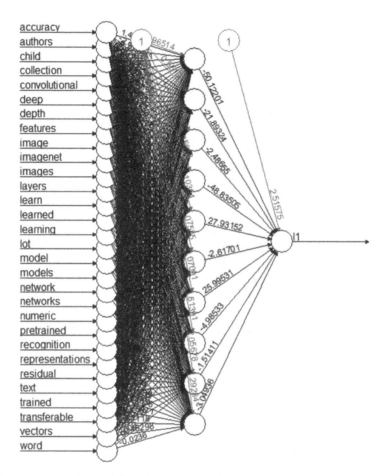

Figure 5.9 Neural network for subset 1 (screen shot).
Source: G. Singh Bawa.

expected to be similar to the one from the entire data set. The ranks in Table 5.18 are with respect to original SVD weights.

It can be observed that for both the subsets, the top 20 terms explain about 80 percent of variability of the target variable. However, as shown in Table 5.19, subset 2 has almost all of its top 10 terms as overlapping with the "topic 3" terms.

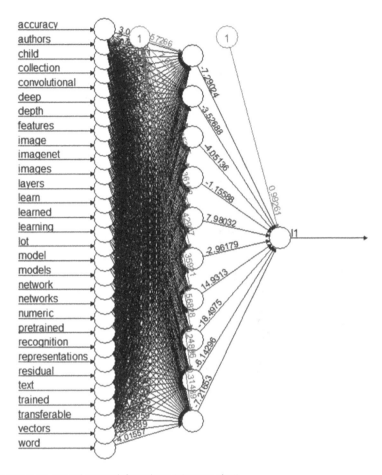

Figure 5.10 Neural network for subset 2 (screen shot).
Source: G. Singh Bawa.

It is noteworthy that the top five terms in subset 2 are either ranked toward the bottom of subset 1 or do not occur in its top 20. This illustrates that subsets themselves have an individuality that can displace the distribution of topics when compared to the original host population. Consequently, terms that describe the general topic may not accurately describe the component subsets.

Table 5.18 Relative Ranked Importance of Terms in Respective Subsets

Subset 1 Hypernyms	Relative importance	Rank	Subset 2 Hypernyms	Relative importance	Rank
recognition	5%	17	authors	6%	19
Deep	5%	11	features	5%	3
Learning	5%	10	image	5%	30
Models	5%	7	numeric	5%	2
Images	4%	27	model	5%	1
Network	4%	28	models	4%	7
transferable	4%	16	word	4%	9
Imagenet	4%	18	vectors	4%	13
Accuracy	4%	24	learning	4%	10
Text	4%	5	deep	4%	11
Vectors	4%	13	collection	4%	23
Word	4%	9	text	4%	5
Trained	3%	6	child	4%	22
Learn	3%	26	transferable	3%	16
Authors	3%	19	network	3%	28
Networks	3%	8	recognition	3%	17
Pretrained	3%	4	networks	3%	8
Residual	3%	14	representations	3%	20
Features	3%	3	lot	3%	29
Image	3%	30	trained	3%	6
Collection	3%	23	learn	3%	26
Layers	3%	25	convolutional	2%	21
Child	3%	22	images	2%	27
Lot	2%	29	pretrained	2%	4
Model	2%	1	imagenet	2%	18
Learned	2%	15	accuracy	2%	24
Numeric	2%	2	residual	2%	14
convolutional	2%	21	depth	2%	12
depth	2%	12	layers	2%	25
representations	2%	20	learned	2%	15

Table 5.19 Top Terms in Respective Subsets

Subset 1	Subset 1 order	Subset 2	Subset 2 order (term in subset 1)
Recognition	1	authors	15
Deep	2	features	19
Learning	3	image	20
Models	4	numeric	
Images	5	model	
Network	6	models	4
transferable	7	word	12
Imagenet	8	vectors	11
Accuracy	9	learning	3
Text	10	deep	2
Vectors	11	collection	
Word	12	text	10
Trained	13	child	
Learn	14	transferable	7
Authors	15	network	6
Networks	16	recognition	1
Pretrained	17	networks	16
Residual	18	representations	
Features	19	lot	
Image	20	trained	13

CONCLUSION

This application demonstrates how an overlay of community-based semantic fields superimposed on text topics can lead to the extraction of unique terms that capture unique meanings for subsets extracted from the text topics themselves.

This finding has been used as the basis for a patent on the use characteristics of the SAS Topic Node display.[xii] It forms the basis of a SAS Global Forum paper.[xiii] The approach relies on first carrying out a vector-based topic identification that is computed across the entire conversational corpus, typically a social media collection (although the effects of this approach are highly visible in social media, we also know that any collection of documents can be seen to represent different communities of authors). In the next step, various social groupings or subnets are identified. Social network membership and role (leader/follower) can be identified so as to weight potential conversational influence. Word and phrase lists can be generated for each of the topic scores in each of the social groupings. The word and phrase lists are identified through rule induction through the use of either machine learning or specialized procedures such as the *Boollear* Boolean rule generator.[xiv] By examining the overlap of common terms for topics among the various subcommunities, we can identify which descriptors apply across all social groups and which specialized, idiosyncratic, and idiomatic descriptors emerge in various subgroups. This approach allows us to automate the identification of synonyms across various contexts in a collection of documents.

NOTES

i. S. Deerwester, S. Dumais, T. Landauer, G. Furnas, and R. Harshman, "Indexing by Latent Semantic Analysis," *Journal of the American Society of Information Science*, 41, no. 6 (1990): 391–407.

ii. D.M. Blei, A.Y. Ng, M.I. Jordan, "Latent Dirichlet Allocation," *Journal of Machine Learning Research* 3 (2003): 993–1022.

iii. J.A. Cox, "The Whats, Whys, and Wherefores of Topic Discovery and Management: Part One," *SAS Voices* (April 16, 2010), https://blogs.sas.com/content/sascom/2010/04/16/the-whats-whys-and-wherefores-of-topic-discovery-and-management-part-one/; and SAS Institute Inc., *Getting Started with SAS® Text Miner 4* (Cary, NC: SAS Institute Inc., 2010).

iv. R. Albright, *Taming Text with the SVD* (Cary, NC: SAS Institute Inc., 2004).

v. R. Albright, J. Cox, and K. Daly, "Skinning the Cat: Comparing Alternative Text Mining Algorithms for Categorization," *Proceedings of the 2nd Data Mining Conference of DiaMondSUG*, DM Paper 113. (Chicago, IL: DiaMondSUG, 2001).

vi. SAS Institute Inc., *SAS Enterprise Miner 15.1: Reference Help* (Cary, NC: SAS Institute Inc., 2018).

vii. J.A. Cox, "Topic Advice about Topics, Redux," *SAS Voices* (October 26, 2015). https://blogs.sas.com/content/sascom/2015/10/26/topical-advice-about-topics-redux/.

viii. D.M. Blei, A.Y. Ng, and M.I. Jordan, "Latent Dirichlet Allocation," *Journal of Machine Learning Research* 3 (2003): 993–1022.

ix. I.B. Myers, *The Myers-Briggs Type Indicator: Manual* (Consulting Psychologists Press, 1962). https://doi.org/10.1037/14404-000.

x. J. Leskovec, L. Backstrom, and J.M. Kleinberg, "Meme-Tracking and the Dynamics of the News Cycle, KDD '09," *Proceedings of the 15th ACM SIGKDD international Conference on Knowledge Discovery and Data Mining*, 2009, 497–506. https://doi.org/10.1145/1557019.1557077.

xi. https://www.kaggle.com/canggih/voted-kaggle-dataset.

xii. J. Cox, B. deVille, and Z. Zhao, "Generating and Displaying Canonical Rule Sets with Dimensional Targets," US Patent (2017). US 9582761 B2.

xiii. G. Bawa, B. deVille, S. Shenoy, and K. Pakira, *Fine Tuning Topical Content in Written Expression in Cloud-based Environments*, SAS Global Forum, Paper 2070-2018. (Cary, NC: SAS Institute Inc., 2018). https://www.sas.com/content/dam/SAS/support/en/sas-global-forum-proceedings/2018/2070-2018.pdf.

xiv. J. Cox and Z. Zhao, "System for Efficiently Generating k-Maximally Predictive Association Rules with a Given Consequent," US Patent (2014). US 20140337271.

CHAPTER **6**

Classification
and Prediction

USE CASE SCENARIO

Here we consider repairs under warranty for a global truck manufacturer. In this situation, the manufacturer is trying to get a more accurate warranty repair report, as better accuracy drives better manufacturing processes in the future. The current situation relies on relatively short, cryptic texts left by mechanics. Manual spot checks have demonstrated that the text that is entered carries an inaccurate warranty code about 50 percent of the time. The main goal is to associate mechanics notes with actual repairs undertaken. This can lead to better ways of assigning warranty codes that more accurately reflect actual repairs. We developed a text analytics-based prediction and deployment application for the truck manufacturer. This work was documented in two successive SAS User Conferences presentations.[i]

Currently, the warranty claim process at this vehicle manufacturer assigns a warranty type/cause (WTC) code to warranty claims (this is an eight-digit code). This system, carried out by human operators, had been in production for 15 years and has been audited and verified to produce an approximately 50 percent accuracy rate to claim type.

This system and the claim type/cause assignment also form the basis for the quality targets that are set for the vehicle manufacturing division.

The main goal of the analysis was to conduct a specific proof of concept and financial impact analysis to determine whether there is enough characteristic information in the current warranty claim records to automate the WTC code assignment process. This would save time and costs and would also contribute to the establishment of a more reproducible code-assignment process.

The attributes of this proof of concept are as follows:

1. Pick 12 WTC codes (out of the total 7500+ codes) that are most prevalent and that, when automated, would likely yield the greatest benefits and potential cost savings.

2. Use a combination of current structured numeric fields and free-form text fields to develop a WTC code outcome predictive model that is subject to an independent data set verification process.

Table 6.1 Record Layout of Warranty Action with FAILDES Text Target Field

CHASSIS	CH613
MILES	156060
PLACEDTE	6/4/2003
DELDATE	2/18/2004
CLAIMDTE	5/19/2004
MOS	8
PLANT	50
TOTCREDT	$501
CLAIMTYP	3912-992001
FAILCODE	C639
FAILDES	SLACK PI 561 FAN HAD EXCESSIVE SLACK. REPLACED FAN HUB

3. Demonstrate code prediction validation – based on the independent data – that is at least as good as human code assignment validation (currently in the 50 percent range).

The approach outlined in (2) above recognizes that the warranty repair is not simply a function of the descriptive notes and is also affected by such vehicle characteristics as miles driven, even manufacturing location. This supplementary information can be used to supplement the text notes in arriving at a more accurate warranty code prediction model.

Requirement (3) led to the development of a prediction/classification model. This model took advantage of the superior predictive capabilities of multiagent models, developed with multiple decision trees. By using the combination of qualitative data based on text and quantitative data based on the numeric fields in the warranty records, we were able to get the best predictive results possible.

Table 6.1 shows a typical record layout and example text entry – shown in the *FAILDES* field.

Composite Document Construction

At the outset, we assembled a data set that contained a selected range of warranty codes to serve as the target to be predicted where each record contained the target code and a number of fields that would serve as the predictors.

Target Codes

There were over 1900 eight-digit warranty codes contained in the data set that was used in this initial exercise. There were over 600,000 records available for the analysis (an average of about 300 records per code). For the proof-of-concept task we picked 12 warranty codes for our initial set of analyses. These were the codes that are most prevalent and that, when automated, would be likely to yield the greatest benefits and potential cost savings.

The test scenario is shown in Figure 6.1. Each record contains a target field, multiple variables extracted from the warranty record, and, finally, singular value decomposition (SVD) constructs created from the text analytics processing of the extracted text field taken from the warranty action record.

The warranty codes that were used as training targets are shown in Table 6.2. To ensure that the sampled data used in the analysis

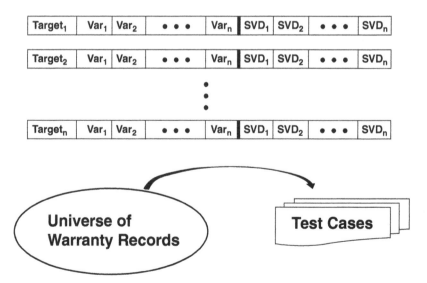

Figure 6.1 Test scenario record structure illustration.
Source: B. deVille.

Table 6.2 Claim Code Distributions in Host and Sample Data Sets

	Before Sampling		After Sampling	
Code	Frequency	Percent	Frequency	Percent
Air Compressor	376	0.05%	376	0.32%
Alternator	4755	0.68%	4755	4.06%
Axle Cross Steering	76	0.01%	76	0.06%
Battery	3221	0.46%	3221	2.75%
Brake Lines/Clamps/Fittings	7123	1.02%	7123	6.09%
Fan Drive	9234	1.32%	9234	7.89%
Fuel Tank	4432	0.64%	4432	3.79%
Heater A/C Panel	6467	0.93%	6467	5.53%
Piping Connect/Fit	5405	0.78%	5405	4.62%
Starter	2997	0.43%	2997	2.56%
Wire Cab to Chassis	7778	1.12%	7778	6.65%
Other	645441	92.56%	65146	55.68%
Total	697305		117010	

accurately reflects the host data set, both host data distributions ("the population") and the sample data distributions are shown.

The fixed field data used in generating the predictive models are shown in Table 6.3.

When the FAILDES text fields were rolled up and associated with each service action the resulting aggregated text field was used as a target for the text analytics. This produced 42 unique singular value composites, which were then used as summaries of the text part of the predictions used for the modeling step of the analysis.

Model Development

Preprocess

We began with the development of a term list, synonym list, and start–stop and stemming lists. This information is used to preprocess the text data so as to reduce the complexity and dimensionality of the text and to map the text into a more manageable set of terms.

Table 6.3 Fixed Field Data Used in Prediction

Field	Description
CHASSIS	Vehicle number
PLANT	Plant code
PLACEDTE	Build date
DELIVERY	Delivery date
REPAIRDT	Repair date
CLAIMDTE	Claim date
CLAIMTYP	Type of claim (warranty, prep for delivery)
SERVMOS	Months in service
MILES	Mileage (x 1000)
TOTCREDT	Total credit
FAILPART	Failed part
MICROFSC	Micro film number
RWRNO	Claim number
SEQUENCE	Text sequence number
FAILDES	Claim text

Dimension Reduction

We performed a number of dimensional reduction tasks for the term set using both factor analytic and cluster analysis approaches (as well as both approaches in combination). The goal is to assemble a tractable text term reduced form representation that is predictive of warranty codes. This is an iterative trial-and-error process.

We began by creating the text mining summary model components; here, the important component was the training set of data with the records that consisted of the target value, the quantitative fields extracted from the warranty service records and, finally, the singular value decomposition composites (ultimately, we used 42 SVD constructs).

Modeling

Once a set of reduced form terms was constructed, we built four separate, predictive models using both single model and multiple-model (boosted, bagged) approaches; each model used the service record fields as quantitative input terms, as well as the text-derived SVD quantitative fields on the data records. Four modeling approaches were developed to determine whether the text information added predictive value and whether multiagent modeling approaches would add predictive value.

All results were validated for accuracy through the use of a split-sample train/validation approach, whereby 30 percent of the original data records were set aside to compare predicted results from the model with actual results based on this holdout set of test data. This 70:30 ratio is a classical approach that works well in preserving as much information as possible to train the predictive models while at the same time setting aside enough hold-back information (a 30 percent sample) to effectively rate the validity of the trained models after the fact.

- The first analysis used only the quantitative data fields to produce a predictive classification model for the warranty code.
- The second approach supplemented the quantitative fields with the introduction of the text mining summary predictors (42 dimensional summaries).
- The third approach was based on bagging the combined quantitative and text mining predictors.
- The fourth approach was based on boosting the combined quantitative and text mining predictors.

The predictive models are tuned using a separate validation test sample.

Ensemble or Multiagent Models

Since the mid-1990s, a number of multiple random decision tree approaches have been developed that take advantage of advances in theory and computing power and to increase classification accuracy, including situations with relatively rare codes.[ii] Multiple decision trees are frequently referred to as *forests, bagged, boosted, committee,* or *ensemble* classifiers.

The results of the four analysis scenarios are referenced in the captured response chart shown in Figure 6.2. *Captured response* (or *Lift*) is a common way to assess the performance of a model. It shows how many of the warranty codes on the test data were actually correctly predicted for the percentage of the data records that were processed by the respective scoring models (up to 100 percent shown on the right-hand side of the chart). The vertical axis on the figure shows how many target warranty codes were correctly predicted by the model while the horizontal axis shows the top-performing features of the model ranging from the top 1 percent of the model predictions on the left to weaker and weaker model components, until all model elements are included (shown on the right-hand side of the figure).

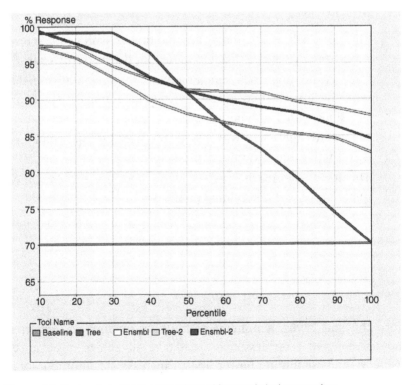

Figure 6.2 Captured response comparison of four analytical approaches.
Source: B. deVille.

The final results were as follows:

Model Scenario	Accuracy
Model with quantitative-only fields (shown as a line, Tree, in Figure 6.2).	70%
Model with a single tree and text and quantitative fields contained in the data (shown as a line, Tree-2, in Figure 6.2).	82%
Model with bagged trees (this includes text and quantitative fields and is shown as a line, Ensmbl-2, in Figure 6.2).	84%
Model with boosted trees (includes text and quantitative fields and is shown as a line, Ensmbl, in Figure 6.2).	87%

All quantitative models perform better than the manual methods that are currently in use (these have a 50 percent accuracy rate). The quantitative, single-equation-only model performs at a 70 percent accuracy rate. When text is added as a predictive input to the model, we get an increase to 82 percent accuracy. Multiagent methods that represent a combination of all quantitative and qualitative prediction information pooled together produce the best results. Because boosting, in particular, is "tuned" to detect rare, difficult-to-classify cases, it is no surprise that the boosting results would produce the best overall results.

These results enable us to move from an overall accuracy rate of about 70 percent with the single-tree (quantitative fields only) model to an accuracy rate that is close to 90 percent with the multitree boosted method. All models outperformed the observed reproducibility rate of only 50 percent that characterizes the current (manual) method of assigning warranty codes.

IDENTIFYING DRIVERS OF TEXTUAL CONSUMER FEEDBACK USING DISTANCE-BASED CLUSTERING AND MATRIX FACTORIZATION

In this use case, we will illustrate how ecommerce platforms can employ analytics to examine consumer reviews pertaining to the products bought from different partner sellers to understand the key reasons driving bad/good reviews.

Use Case Scenario: Retailer Reliability Ecommerce

The objective of the use case is to establish an analytical procedure, which helps in extracting meaningful insights for ecommerce marketers to help in making decisions by applying natural language processing techniques and algorithms to the textual reviews obtained from consumers. These insights from the text analytics exercise will help identify the conversational drivers impacting ratings and reviews in both positive and negative directions and will ultimately aid the business in applying the findings to process improvements in both internal processes and external processes with associated retailers who are shipping the products directly to consumers.

In our use case, we discuss the analytical approaches that foster better understanding of the consumers' outlook with respect to the products sold by the marketers. The insights and information generated is valuable for businesses since it allows them to track the needs of their potential consumer base and helps them in identifying if external retailers and agents are diminishing or improving the brand image. These outcomes help the business to establish long-term and short-term strategies and tactics toward their partner retailers.

Assessment Mechanism

One thing to note is that the reviews and feedback provided by consumers is generally unstructured and in textual format. This leads to the requirement to supplement traditional quantitative approaches with qualitative approaches based on text analytics and natural language processing (NLP). Consumers are often encouraged to allocate a rating in the range of one to five (1–5) stars, which summarizes their overall experience. This rating might not necessarily reflect the psychological state of the consumer when compared to a detailed review of the associated text narrative. Additionally, because the rating scale is not normalized, ratings obtained from different consumers are not reliably comparable. For example, a rating of four stars for Consumer 1 might be equivalent to a rating of five stars for Consumer 2 and three stars for Consumer 3. Hence, to facilitate comparable analysis in our use case, we use the polarity scores from sentiment analysis for all the reviews. Since the same model is used to score each feedback document, the scale of polarity scores between −1 to +1 becomes comparable. We consider text tokens as the feature elements for our analysis. Since tokens are the base-level constituent primitive of reviews, they are considered to reflect the true conversational drivers through their occurrences across all review documents. Instead of using unigrams to represent these tokens, we use bigrams as they provide a richer input stream. In terms of token (bigram) weights, we use the *Term Frequency–Inverse Document Frequency (TF-IDF)* score since these scores accommodate both frequency and specificity of the tokens across each document over the entire data set. Finally, we construct a Boolean document model using the high-TF-IDF tokens to obtain the conversational drivers, which are driving the reviews toward a negative/positive sentiment.

Our use case has the following structure:

- We provide a literature review of various treatments of customer feedback to extract contextual information about the techniques and methodology used in our use case.
- We then introduce the business problem of our experimental research along with the associated data we will be using for our analysis to illustrate the benefit of our analytical methodology.
- In data preparation and exploratory analysis, we discuss the various NLP and text mining techniques we employ to extract, process, and collate the data, converting it from textual unstructured format to a numeric structured suitable for model input.
- In a section on experimental analysis and document modeling we show the experimental findings from the exploratory data analysis and use it to build the Boolean document model – a prescriptive model that helps in generating the key drivers of reviews that characterize negative and positive sentiment.
- In the final concluding section, we discuss how the insights can be interpreted and translated to understand how third-party retailer stakeholders may affect product perceptions.

A Review of the Literature on Analyzing Customer Feedback

Research and development work with the aim to analyze web-based customer feedback is a popular area of text mining. Many studies have been completed and published. For example, Amato et al. implemented an efficient apparatus for text preprocessing where each linguistic token is allotted a weight, which is computed using the TF-IDF formula.[iii] Sentiment analysis and opinion mining are key areas of interest in the examination of consumer-generated content.[iv] The research by Hu et al.[v] and Gupta et al.[vi] discusses how NLP techniques can be used to establish noun–adjective pairs from documents using parts-of-speech (POS) tagging.

These extracted text artifacts can be then used as input to create an association rule-mining model that associates user feedback to product attributes. Chinsa shows how linguistic rules and sentiment analysis can be used to analyze consumer feedback and identify opinion direction and other important characteristics about businesses.[vii] Another model put forward by Titov et al., known as the Multi-Aspect Sentiment (MAS) model, deals with unlocking latent topics in consumer feedback, thereby extracting portions of the text which link to the assessment aspect that forms the rating scale.[viii] Yahav et al. propose a modification to TF-IDF that considers an introduction of a bias correction that is more appropriate for social media frameworks.[ix]

One of the primary sources of motivation for this use case was the idea and initial set of findings offered in Korfiatis et al.,[x] which talks about the relationship between various components of a feedback data set, such as review texts and rating scores. One other hypothesis was articulated in Lackermair et al.[xi] This asserts that reviews and feedback obtained on online platforms are important foundations for information with respect to consumer engagement. Another novel unsupervised analytical procedure for opinion mining, focusing on web-based content, was proposed by Colhon et al.[xii] The authors proposed that reviews from travelers visiting different destinations could be mined with an unsupervised methodology for sentiment analysis that could be used to identify keywords to define the basis of a set of domain-specific *seed* words in feedback documents. Another source of inspiration, proposed by Cambria et al., was a sentiment analysis algorithm that does not have a requirement of training.[xiii] The researchers utilize English grammatical rules in determining the document polarity measure. Each of these rules were associated with a trigger – once a trigger in the document is fired then a rule is launched that returns a partial polarity measure. Our research further draws inspiration from the sentiment analysis methodology that attempts to establish the polarity of a precise latent topic instead of the entire document text, as proposed by Nasukawa and Yi.[xiv] Deploying a wide range of analytics to make strategies targeted to having better partner retailers for ecommerce businesses is discussed by Polina et al.[xv]

Business Problem and Data Introduction

The example illustrated in the following sections of the use case consists of a sample of ecommerce feedback data for a range of products sold by two different retailers. Our objective is to employ text analytics and NLP techniques to identify key conversational drivers of the textual feedback data and to understand if they are driving the consumers' perception in a negative or positive way.

Table 6.4 shows a view of the data set that is being considered. The fields are shown in Table 6.5.

Data Preparation and Exploratory Analysis

There are a number of approaches to scanning text and identifying components through tokenization. In our case possible granularities include word level, *n*-gram level, sentence level or even paragraph level to identify "terms." In this case, we elected to include *n-grams*; here they are especially useful since they can automatically record negative sentiments (as reflected, for example, in the *n*-gram "not very helpful"). In the preprocessing we did not use negation stop words so as to enable us to capture negative senses (if negative stop words had been used, then the negation operator would have been excluded from the analysis).

Table 6.4 Sample Data from Amazon

User Id	Product Name	Review Text	Rating	Retailer_Id
HTC1217284	PID_001	Works amazing for people with oily skin	5	76s34kiut
eyj7I9svffi4I7	PID_001	Amazing wipes. Leaves skin smooth.	5	76s34kiut
HTC999619	PID_001	My daughter actually tried these	5	qcs56ty
HTC1277819	PID_001	I love these wipes. They take off	5	qcs56ty
HTC1421410	PID_001	It works wonderfully!	5	76s34kiut
HTC1651481	PID_001	This used to be my favorite face cleaner.	2	76s34kiut

Table 6.5 Field Descriptors Amazon Feedback Data

User_Id	The identification key of the consumers who provided the feedback.
Product_Name	The product names reviewed.
Review_Text	Primary field – detailed textual reviews.
Rating	Self-assigned product rating
Retailer_Id	Two distinct IDs for different retail partners

Once we include our features for the model, we try to identify how each of them is relevant or important across the set of consumer reviews by providing weights for them. As discussed in the chapter on preprocessing, TF-IDF weights are a useful statistical metric that can help in evaluating the importance of a token to a specific document in a collection of documents, or corpus. This measure of importance is defined in such a manner that it increases in proportion to the frequency of a token within the document and is penalized by the occurrence in the corpus across all the documents.

The reason for choosing the TFIDF measure in our illustration is that we want to look at those tokens that are both frequent across documents in the corpus and that have a high level of specificity. Table 6.6

Table 6.6 Top Bigrams from Feedback in Retailer 1

healthier options	everyday use	nothing noticeable
bad rash	acne worsened	very dry
fresher clear	really bad	immediately improved
horrible allergic	manufacturing needs	bottle lids
skin broke	too thick	package was
never received	broken off	premium product
non comedogenic	welts appeared	are working
was recommended	stopped stocking	skin clear
never delivered	was broken	allergic reaction
review parabens	stores stopped	terrible customer
not greasy	customer service	15 years

shows the top few bigrams identified from the feedback obtained for retailer 1. Table 6.7 shows the bigrams taken from feedback associated with transactions for retailer 2.

We see that majority of top bigrams are associated with a negative sentiment for both the retailers. This can be validated by analyzing

Table 6.7 Top Bigrams from Feedback in Retailer 2

itchy skin	highly recommended	improved formula
the sun	so lightweight	absolutely terrible
slight redness	used rainbath	about 2 weeks
causes breakouts	great mascara	slightly refreshing
feels nice	extremely flaky	good cleanser
inactive ingredients	would recommend	so intoxicating
great sunscreen	smells nice	includes sunscreens
greasy perfumed	extremely harmful	severe tingling
puffiness after	eyes water	hydrated completely
magic mask	red rash	the protection
sun protection	working instantly	barely visible
extremely swollen		

Table 6.8 Average Sentiment Polarity of Customer Feedback

	average sentiment polarity
retailer 1	−0.2417
retailer 2	−0.1902
overall	−0.21595

their average sentiment scores. We noticed that the average sentiment is a little less negative for retailer 2, as shown in Table 6.8.

We can verify the extent and importance of these top bigrams in driving the overall sentiment of reviews by using them as features in a Boolean document model. This is taken up in the next section.

Experimental Analysis and Document Modeling

In this section, we model the features obtained from the preliminary analysis in the previous section. We use a binary target variable that reflects whether the review or feedback is a positive or negative sentiment. We adapt a standard text classification task with some modifications: text classification, ideally, is an exercise where the objective is to categorize document instances depending on the terms/tokens they are built from. Rather than construct a classification model with the goal of assigning a class or category, we use a predictive model where we estimate the probability of a given class membership.

Text classification models often do not employ any context, since, in most of the cases, they are based on a bag-of-words, where there is no sense of ordering of contents. In our example, we will explicitly introduce the notion of conditional probability to determine the strength of association between a term pair – or bigram – and the sentiment. In this task, we can harness conditional probability (or Bayes' theorem) to categorize a document D into category 1 or 2, for example, depending on the posterior conditional probability of Probability (Category 1 | D) and Probability (Category 2 | D); that is, any document will be classified to a category, depending on which posterior probability is maximum. In our illustration, let's say the binomial target variable 0–1 signifies if a document is positive sentiment or negative sentiment.

Now, if we use the tokens obtained earlier as features that characterize the documents, then we have a similar classification exercise. However, we are not concerned about the task of predictive classification and want to focus on the explicit importance of each of the feature bigram tokens in the model; that is, instead of using the model to predict unknown text instances, our objective is to observe the behavior of the features while constructing the best-fit model.

In terms of modeling the documents, we use the Bernoulli setup. A Bernoulli document model is one where a document has a representation feature vector consisting of binary rudiments that assume values of 0 and 1 depending on absence or presence of the token. For our experiment (Table 6.9), this translates to creating a matrix where documents signify rows and bigram tokens as columns with 1–0 values populated in the cells based on the bigram tokens' presence or absence across documents.

As discussed earlier, in the setting of the Bernoulli document model, the representation of a document is done using a binary vector, which ideally denotes a point in the space generated by the tokens present in the corpus. Let's say the corpus consists of vocabulary V

Table 6.9 Example Input Matrix for the Boolean Document Model

	healthier options	everyday use	nothing noticeable	was recommend	stopped stocking
document 1	0	0	0	1	0
document 2	1	0	0	0	1
document 3	1	1	0	1	0
document 4	0	0	0	0	0
document 5	0	0	0	0	0
document 6	1	0	0	1	1
document 7	1	1	1	0	0
document 8	1	0	1	1	0
document 9	1	0	1	1	0
document 10	0	1	1	1	0
document 11	0	0	0	1	1
document 12	0	1	0	0	0

having a set of $|V|$ tokens, then the tth element of a document vector is in correspondence to token w_t in the vocabulary. Let the feature vector for the document D be represented by b; the tth element of b, expressed as b_t, assumes the value 0 or 1, depending on the occurrence of term w_t in the document.

Let $P(w_t|C_k)$ be the probability of token w_t existing in a document belonging to category k and $(1 - P(w_t|C_k))$ signify the probability of absence of token w_t. Then, on making the underlying assumptions of naïve Bayes that these probabilities of every token existing in a document are independent of the existence of the other tokens, then the document likelihood $P(D|C)$ as a function of the individual word likelihoods $P(w_t|C_k)$ is:

$$P\left(D|C_k\right) = P\left(\mathbf{b}|C_k\right) = \prod_{t=1}^{|V|}\left[b_t P\left(w_t|C_k\right) + \left(1 - b_t\right)\left(1 - P\left(w_t|C_k\right)\right)\right]$$

The above expression is an iterative product over all tokens existing in the corpus. If token w_t exists, then b_t equals 1 and the associated probability is $P(w_t|C_k)$. Similarly, if the token w_t is absent, then b_t equals 0 and the required probability is $1 - P(w_t|C_k)$. This can be thought of as a model that generates document feature vectors pertaining to category k where the document feature vector is expressed as a set of weighted coin tosses of cardinality $|V|$, with success probability equaling $P(w_t|C_k)$.

Even though the primary objective while fitting a naïve Bayes' model is to classify unseen text using the model by calculating the posterior category probabilities, we are going to focus more on the feature conditional probability $P(w_t|C_k)$. This measure reflects the strength of effect of features for each category in question. In our case, if we focus on the negative category (where feedback documents are negative), this probability measure will give a comparative idea of the explanatory power of each of the feature bigram tokens we have shortlisted. We have shown the values in Tables 6.10 and 6.11 with the aim of comparing the tokens among themselves as to which of them are more aligned to documents that carry a negative sentiment.

Table 6.10 Feature Probabilities
with Respect to Negative Assessment,
Retailer 1

bigram	$P\,(w_t\,|C_k)$
acne worsened	0.035
customer service	0.0344
very dry	0.034
broken off	0.0333
terrible customer	0.03311
non comedogenic	0.0331
welts appeared	0.033
immediately improved	0.032
skin broke	0.0311
bad rash	0.031
never delivered	0.03
review parabens	0.029
stopped stocking	0.029
horrible allergic	0.028
manufacturing needs	0.0277
not greasy	0.02
skin clear	0.019
healthier options	0.016

The findings help in understanding the extent to which the most frequent and specific bigram tokens selected earlier behave in explaining the ability to categorize or identify negative sentiment feedback. As a result, the business can use these insights to understand whether the tokens that drive the feedback are having a negative or positive impact as well as the extent of the impact. Further, the ecommerce business can strategize depending on whether the identified driver of feedback is due to a production, design, or product attribute issue or is likely the result of the third-party retailer stakeholder.

Table 6.11 Feature Probabilities
with Respect to Negative Assessment,
Retailer 2

bigram	$P(w_t|C_k)$
absolutely terrible	0.0399
causes breakouts	0.03984
itchy skin	0.03915
working instantly	0.03884
eyes water	0.03819
slightly refreshing	0.03793
hydrated completely	0.03776
slight redness	0.03742
extremely flaky	0.0373
barely visible	0.03672
severe tingling	0.03656
red rash	0.03648
inactive ingredients	0.03625
improved formula	0.0362
extremely swollen	0.03535
so lightweight	0.03515
sun protection	0.0241
great sunscreen	0.0211
good cleanser	0.0187

Discussion

Reviews posted on web platforms by consumers have become a significant source of information through which consumers can express associated experiences and views about the products and services that they have consumed. It is a text-based communication system with significant potential in providing new perceptions, and it potentially facilitates a number of marketing opportunities. When marketers read through the reviews posted by consumers, it gives them a platform to listen closely to customer sentiment with respect to the perception of their own consumer base. Feedback received from consumers are beneficial for businesses to identify its strong and weak points, and thus use the insights to strategically cultivate ideas that improve its brand value through improvement in products and services.

At a high level, the ecommerce business can quickly assess from the sentiment scores that the product in our experiment is not generating much positive feedback from consumers. As we see here, most of the drivers that emerged from the model that have higher association to the negative consumer feedback are product oriented. These drivers are almost uniformly distributed between the consumer feedback coming from both the retailers. This indicates that the product level issues which the consumers do not exist regardless of retailer. Yet one of the retailers attracted more negative sentiment. If we look at the drivers for retailer 1 (Table 6.10), in addition to product level issues like ingredients, effects after usage, we see some additional issues such as "customer service," "never delivered," and "stopped stocking." These additional drivers are entirely third-party retailer oriented and are present only for retailer 1 and almost none for retailer 2 (Table 6.11). Thus, the ecommerce business can identify the issues pertaining to the third-party retailers that are involved in substandard operations and is low on reliability.

NOTES

i. B. deVille, "Text Mining with "Holographic" Decision Tree Ensembles," Paper 72-31, SUGI 31, *SAS User's Group International Conference, Paper 084-2007*, San Francisco (Cary, NC: SAS Institute Inc., 2006). www2.sas.com/proceedings/sugi31/072-31 .pdf; and B. deVille, *Ubiquitous Scoring of 1000+ Warranty Categories Using Prediction Rules Derived from Text*, SAS Global Forum, Paper 084-2007 (Cary, NC: SAS Institute Inc., 2007), www2.sas.com/proceedings/forum2007/084-2007.pdf.

ii. Y. Amit and D. Geman, "Shape Quantization and Recognition with Randomized Trees," *Neural Computation* 9 (1996, 1997): 1545–1588; L. Breiman, "Bagging Predictors," *Machine Learning* 24, no. 2 (1996): 123–140; L. Breiman, "Arcing Classifiers," *The Annals of Statistics* 26, no. 3 (1998): 801–849; and Y. Freund and R. E. Schapire, "A Decision-theoretic Generalization of On-line Learning and an Application to Boosting," *Proceedings of the 2nd European Conference on Computational Learning Theory* (Barcelona, Spain: Eurocolt95, 1995), 23–37.

iii. F. Amato, V. Moscato, A. Picariello, and G. Sperl, "Diffusion Algorithms in Multimedia Social Networks: A Preliminary Model," *Proceedings of the IEEE/ACM International Conference on Advances in Social Networks Analysis and Mining* (Sydney, Australia: IEEE, 31 July–3 August 2017), 844–851.

iv. O. Müller, M. Fay, and J. V. Brocke, "The Effect of Big Data and Analytics on Firm Performance: An Econometric Analysis Considering Industry Characteristics," *J. Manag. Inf. Syst.* 35 (2018): 488–509.

v. M. Hu and B. Liu, "Mining and Summarizing Customer Reviews," *KDD '04: Proceedings of the Tenth ACM SIGKDD International Conference on Knowledge Discovery and Data Mining* (New York: ACM, 2004), pp. 168–177.

vi. A. Gupta, T. Tenneti, and A. Gupta, "Sentiment based Summarization of Restaurant Reviews, *Final Year Project* (2009), www.academia.edu/download/53603548/9.pdf (accessed December 10, 2020).

vii. T. C. Chinsa and J. Shibily, "Aspect-based Opinion Mining from Restaurant Reviews," *International Journal of Computer Applications* 975 (2014): 8887, and *Advanced Computing and Communication Techniques for High Performance Applications* (ICACCTHPA-2014), https://research.ijcaonline.org/icaccthpa2014/number1/icaccthpa6002.pdf

viii. I. Titov and R. McDonald, "A Joint Model of Text and Aspect Ratings for Sentiment Summarization," *Proceedings of ACL-08* (HLT, 2018), 308–316.

ix. I. Yahav, O. Shehory, and D. Schwartz, "Comments Mining with TF-IDF: The Inherent Bias and Its Removal," *IEEE Trans. Knowl. Data Eng.* 31 (2019): 437–450.

x. N. Korfiatis, P. Stamolampros, P. Kourouthanassis, and V. Sagiadinos, "Measuring Service Quality from Unstructured Data: A Topic Modeling Application on Airline Passengers' Online Reviews," *Expert Syst. Appl.* 116 (2019): 472–486.

xi. G. Lackermair, D. Kailer, and K. Kanmaz, "Importance of Online Product Reviews from a Consumer's Perspective," *Advances in Economics and Business* 1, no. 1 (2013): 1–5.

xii. M. Colhon, C. Badic, and A. Sendre, "Relating the Opinion Holder and the Review Accuracy in Sentiment Analysis of Tourist Reviews," *International Conference on Knowledge Science, Engineering and Management, KSEM'2014*, Lecture Notes in Computer Science, vol. 8793 (New York: Springer, 2014), 246–257.

xiii. E. Cambria and A. Hussain, "Sentic Computing: A Common-Sense-Based Framework for Concept-Level Sentiment Analysis," *Cogn Comput, Springer* 7 (2015): 183–185, DOI 10.1007/s12559-015-9325-0.

xiv. T. Nasukawa and J. Yi, "Sentiment Analysis: Capturing Favorability Using Natural Language Processing," *Proceedings of the 2nd International Conference on Knowledge Capture* (2003): 70–77.

xv. F. Polina, N. Kryvinska, and C. Strauss, "E-Commerce and B2B Services Enterprises," *Advanced Information Networking and Applications, AINA* (2013): 1141–1146.

CHAPTER **7**

Boolean Methods of Classification and Prediction

RULE-BASED TEXT CLASSIFICATION AND PREDICTION

The Boolean rule process, named *Boollear*, in a Cox and Zhao (2014) patent[i] that describes the origination of the approach, was a significant step forward in facilitating the interoperability of manually produced linguistic rules and numerically derived, statistically computed rules. The Boollear process works like traditional decision tree processes so that the process data is run against a target category and a set of predictive/classification rules are extracted. Because the terms of the expression consist of word-terms linked by Boolean operators such as "and," "or," and "not" they can be directly converted to linguistic rules and can therefore be used by a linguistic rules engine.

Whereas common predictive engines like traditional decision trees are limited to Boolean expressions that consist of "and," and "or" operators, Boollear also uses the "not" operator. The "not" operator is a necessary tool in linguistic disambiguation; i.e. the process of specifying the semantic meaning of a word based on the specific context of the word in a sentence. So, for example, the word "bass" in a sentence could be either a bass instrument or bass line in music or it could be a type of fish. A simple disambiguation would look for the presence of "bass" and the absence of "fish" in a sentence to potentially indicate the musical sense of the term. This disambiguation has value in predictive operations that contribute to the accuracy and validity of Boollear predictions. Zhao et al.[ii] demonstrated that rule-based Boollear models can outperform standard predictive engines such as linear support vector machines (SVM).

One example of a set of rule expressions to identify documents relating to bank interest is shown as follows:

(cut $\wedge$ rate $\wedge$ bank $\wedge$ percent $\wedge$ ~sell)	or
(market $\wedge$ money $\wedge$ ~year $\wedge$ percent $\wedge$ ~sale)	or
(repurchase $\wedge$ fee)	or
(rate $\wedge$ prime rate)	or
(federal $\wedge$ rate $\wedge$ maturity)	

In this example, $\wedge$ indicates a logical "and," and ~ indicates a logical negation. The first line of the rule set says that if a document contains the terms "cut," "rate," "bank," and "percent," but does not contain the term "sell," it belongs to the bank interest category. Here we see one of the distinctive characteristics of this set of rules in that the negation operator is also used. This is due to the iterative and heuristic nature of the algorithm that uses both presence and absence of terms in the training data set as preconditions to build the rule. We can easily see an advantage of this representation is that both presence and absence of attributes in the predictive rule are given, an important difference with respect to predictive rules derived from classical predictive models such as decision trees, for example.

Method Description

The operation of the Boollear rule production procedure is outlined in various SAS documentation sources.[iii] As described in the original Cox and Zhao patent and supporting documentation, the Boollear process consists of a term ensemble process that is embedded in a rule ensemble process. A number of heuristic techniques have been evolved to select term combinations to form high-performing rules that attempt to improve both precision and accuracy. An overall estimate called the *F1 score* is also used to ensure that rules that identify small subsets are not penalized with respect to rules that identify large subsets. The F1 score is a better measurement than typical accuracy and precision measures when the data are imbalanced; i.e., with a rare target, because classifiers can obtain high accuracies in unbalanced data simply by predicting that all instances belong to the majority category.

The F1 statistic calculation is as follows (where TP means *true positive* and FP means *false negative*):

$$precision = \frac{TP}{TP + FP}$$

$$recall = \frac{TP}{TP + FN}$$

$$F_1 = 2 * \frac{precision * recall}{precision + recall}$$

- **Term ensemble process.** The overall process works as a standard target estimation procedure where initially all term-target associations are calculated and high-value terms are taken as predictors either singly or in combination with all other terms (either as presence or absence conditions). A g-score information gain measure[iv] is used to measure the term-target association. (The g-score is also known as the likelihood ratio or maximum likelihood statistical significance test.) The rule construction process continues until no more terms can be added (or subtracted) to increase information gain. Once the best rule is selected using this process, the term ensemble loop is closed off, the rule is selected, and the training set is adjusted by removing all documents that conform to that rule.

- **Rule ensemble process.** The new, smaller training set consists of documents that were not covered by the rule that was selected in the term ensemble process. Rules are successively created from each iteration of the training documents. Thus, with each successive rule the resulting training set of documents is reduced in size. One of the strengths of the Boollear algorithm is that smoothing operations are used in computing *estimated precision* of a given rule to adjust and normalize all rule operations even when rules are constructed from smaller and smaller numbers of associated training objects. At some point, the estimated precision falls below a threshold and the process stops. This happens if adding the current best rule does not improve its F1 score.

Characteristics of Boolean Rule Methods

Boolean rule expressions offer a range of advantages beyond the interoperability with linguistic rules. Zhao et al.[v] provide a detailed discussion of the challenges of predicting, or classifying, the taxonomy entries in large text corpora that contain hierarchies of millions or even billions of documents. Most classifier-predictors are top-down models, such as a decision tree, or linear-numerical approaches, called *flat models*, typically variants of standard linear models such as multiple regression. At the time of this writing, they noted that Wikipedia contained 2,365,432 documents organized under a hierarchy with 325,056 categories.

In the Wikipedia example, over 90 percent of the categories contain fewer than 50 documents, less than 0.002 percent of the training data, a substantially unbalanced, rare target. The divide and conquer approach of *Boollear* overcomes the difficulty that linear or flat models encounter when faced with accurately characterizing a rare target. Because the algorithms are implemented as set operations, they are also extremely efficient, so can be readily adapted to handle very large-scale problems. To ensure the accuracy and validity of the model, the Boollear algorithm employs the g-test as an information gain criterion to include terms in the search space and as a test of significance for the resulting rule.

EXAMPLE OF BOOLEAN RULES APPLIED TO TEXT MINING VACCINE DATA

The Vaccine Adverse Event Reporting System (VAERS)[vi] is used to report on adverse drug reactions once a vaccine drug is formally approved and is then distributed to the population on an unrestricted basis. So VAERS is a postclinical trials vaccine safety monitoring system. It is managed by the US Centers for Disease Control and Prevention (CDC) and the US Food and Drug Administration (FDA). People who experience a reaction after a vaccination can visit the VAERS website to log an incident report. The reports are reviewed to determine if there are significant issues with vaccines that have been assessed to be ready for general use in the population. The data are made available for analysis and consist of entries for the patient's attributes such as age and gender, symptoms experienced, and whether the incident was serious or not. An example of the information recorded in the VAERS database is shown in Table 7.1.

The first record shown in Table 7.1 contains the text:

*"Information has been received from an **NP** concerning a 29-year-old-female **pt** who on an unspecified date was vaccinated with varicella virus vaccine live."*

Here we see the *NP* (nurse practitioner) and *pt* (Patient) abbreviations have not been mapped yet. We see that the incident records the

Table 7.1 Example VAERS Data

Symptom Text	Age	Sex	Serious
Information has been received from an NP concerning a 29-year-old female pt who, on an unspecified date, was vaccinated with varicella virus vaccine live. The NP indicated that the pt was 2 weeks pregnant when she received the vaccination. No adverse experiences were reported. The pt sought unspecified medical attention. Follow-up information was received from a physician assistant who indicated that the pt (gravida 4, para 3) was vaccinated on 9/18/01 with a 1st dose of varicella virus vaccine.	29	F	Y
Cellulitis at administration site.	4	M	Y
Approximately 5 minutes after receiving flu and pneumonia vaccine, pt began hollering, "Oh, Oh my neck is hurting! Feels like a knot in my throat, a medicine taste." Complained of chest pain moving to back and leg numbness.	69	F	N
Demyelinating disease; dizziness, blurred vision; difficulty hearing and walking.	77	M	Y
Immediate pain, redness. In about 1 hour, shot raised about 1 inch round lump and pain continued. In a few hours, 1/3 upper arm turned black and blue and pain continued. Next day and for two additional days, movement in upper right arm caused radiated pain. Lump disappeared in one week. Discoloration faded and disappeared in three weeks.	74	F	N

response to the injection of the live varicella virus vaccine. We also see that the patient was a 74-year-old female. The incident was coded as not serious and, if we look at the note in the incident (in the Symtom-Text field) we can see that the lump disappeared after one week and the discoloration faded after three weeks. The second record notes a cellulitis incident in a four-year-old male, and this is coded as a serious incident.

From this we can see that there are both traditional numeric fields, such as sociodemographic attributes, and qualitative text fields, such as symptom text. Both of these fields can be used to predict whether the incident was determined to be serious.

An Example Analysis

This example utilizes predictive text analytics against the publicly available VAERS dataset to demonstrate how text analytics can add lift to models, as well as highlight how text rules can be generated against a structured data target to characterize the data. The adverse event data is collected from people who have experienced an adverse reaction to vaccines. Most reports come from vaccine manufacturers (42 percent) and health care providers (30 percent). Providers are required to report any contraindicated events for a vaccine or any very serious complications. As a first step to characterizing the text field in the VAERS data we compute an initial text cluster analysis in Figure 7.1. Here we see the original Symptom Text along with the VAERS-provided "Costring." The Costring is a short narrative description provided by reviewers when the original incident report is filed.

The text clustering yielded 25 text clusters. Some examples are shown in the right-hand panel of Figure 7.1. Table 7.2 shows a complete listing of the 25 clusters. Clustering is an unsupervised technique that captures similarities in the text, irrespective of an associated target field.

In addition to the text clusters, we also compute the Boolean rules. They are unlike clusters rules, which are constructed in a supervised process that employs a target field in the construction of each rule expression. In this analysis, there were about 160 Boolean rules generated. Table 7.3 shows some of the Boolean rules extracted from an analysis of the VAERS data set. A number of multiple-expression rules are shown here. In the first and third entries, we can see characteristic examples of the Boolean expressions that include both inclusion and exclusion operators. The third entry shows "unspecified medical attention" as an exclusion coupled with the presence of "month" and "diagnose" as inclusions.

Figure 7.2 gives us an indication of the additional predictive power that is provided by these text products – text clusters as categories and Boolean expressions as rules.

In the predictive models given on the left of Figure 7.2, only numeric or structured data is utilized; here, we can only predict serious adverse events less than half the time. When we add text to the models, as shown in the right-hand panel, we can predict serious events about 80 percent of the time.

Figure 7.3, taken from a SAS® Visual Analytics session, illustrates both the effectiveness of the Boolean rule expressions as predictors

SYMPTOM_TEXT	costring
Information has been received from an R.	ANXIETY CELL
Information has been received from an N.	ABORTION LA...
Memory loss, family loss, Mother and fat...	AMNESIA DEL...
Sabin tri vaccines were not good ones. T...	REACT UNEVAL
Cellulitis at administration site.	CELLULITIS IN...
Approximately 5 minutes after receiving fl...	HYPERTENS H...
Demyelinating disease; dizziness; blurre...	AMBLYOPIA D...
Pt presented to ER complaining of swelli...	EDEMA LARYN...
Immediate pain, redness. In about 1 hour...	ECCHYMOSIS...
Infant had a sudden event with cyanosis,...	BRADYCARDI...
Autistic mannerisms, system "shutdown"...	AUTISM CATA...
Loss of speech and coordination.	COORDINAT A...
Reportedly called in after first dose to rep...	RASH
Rash immediately following 03/21/1997 h...	CONVULS EYE...
Large firm, red region at site of injection.	HYSN INJECT...
The child attorney alleged that his mother	OVERDOSE S...
This report is concerning a 4 month old fe...	CONVULS FEV...
Five to ten minute seizure, generalized.	CONVULS ME...
Fever for 3 days. Emesis (recurrent). E...	FEVER VOMIT
Fever, fussiness, questionable hematuria.	AGITATION FE.
Temp 104.5 within 24 hours of immuniza...	FEVER PHARY...
Five day post vaccination, the patient beg...	ASTHENIA ED...
The patient c/o of pain, erythema, edema...	CELLULITIS E...
Patient experienced a baseball sized ede...	EDEMA LYMP

TextCluster_cluster_	category
23	Alleric Concern Female
23	Alleric Concern Female
13	Misc Diagnosis
23	Alleric Concern Female
10	Injection Site
13	Misc Diagnosis
20	Loss
13	Misc Diagnosis
8	Rash Ache
13	Misc Diagnosis
5	Insufficient Information
20	Loss
23	Alleric Concern Female
18	Hospital Seizure
10	Injection Site
6	Legal Complaint
16	Febrile Seizure
16	Febrile Seizure
7	Antibiotic Cellulitis
13	Misc Diagnosis
21	Febrile Seizure AB
20	Loss
10	Injection Site

Figure 7.1 Results of preliminary text clustering in VAERS incident data.
Source: B. deVille.

Table 7.2 Text Clusters Identified in VAERS Data

Cluster Description	Number
Discharge Benadryl	1
Cellulitis autism	2
Pain numbness weakness	3
Hospitalization	4
Insufficient information	5
Legal complaint	6
Antibiotic cellulitis	7
Rash ache	8
Swelling at site	9
Injection site	10
Death SIDS	11
Death SIDS Prevnar	12
Misc. diagnosis	13
Allergic concern	14
Fever nausea diarrhea blood P	15
Febrile seizure	16
Ache chill fever vomit	17
Hospital seizure	18
Shoulder pain rash redness	19
Loss	20
Febrile seizure AB	21
Cry unresponsive	22
Allergic concern female	23
Hospitalize Prevnar	24
Infant Prevnar	25

in unique segments of the data as well as the explanatory power that is offered.

Looking at the decision tree, we see that all the predictive rules are either clusters (shown as the "category" branch at the top of the tree) or Boolean rules. The lower panel tree map shows us one high-leverage node with 444 cases (out of a total of 21,010), which contain 273 serious

Table 7.3 Boolean Rule (Conjunctions) Derived from VAERS Data

Symptom Text	Costring	Age	Sex	Cluster	Conjunction Rule	Serious Y/N
The pt developed redness, swelling, and soreness reaction. Went to ER on 12/30/01.	EDEMA INJECT SITE HYSN INJECT SITE PAIN INJECT SITE	69	M	Shoulder pain rash redness	Redness & ~receive & ~severe	N
The pt developed muscle and joint pain. Her left wrist was especially sore and swollen area on inner forearm. (Naproxen for 10 days with no results.)	ARTHRALGIA EDEMA MYALGIA	34	F	Shoulder pain rash redness	Swollen area	N
On November 20, 2001, this employee received the flu vaccine. On December 19, 2001, he was diagnosed with GBS. He was hospitalized for one week and is recuperating at home. His completed recovery may take three months.	GUILLAIN BARRE SYND	52	M	Cellulitis autism	Month and unspecified medical attention and diagnose	Y

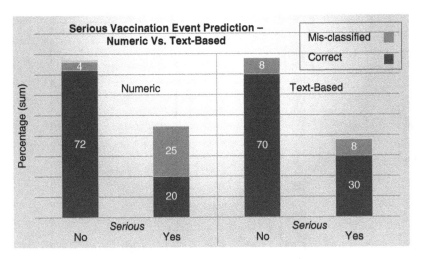

Figure 7.2 Accuracy comparison of numeric data vs. text data model.
Source: B. deVille.

responses (this is about 60% serious cases in this node compared to the overall serious response rate of about 25%).

The category is Febrile Seizure AB (autobody) or Hospital Seizure. A febrile seizure sometimes occurs in children as a result of an infection, including a reaction to a vaccination.

The Boolean rule provides a detailed description of the conditions that are detected that describe this high incidence of serious cases. Since, the "hospital" term occurs in all rules, it also allows us to surmise that there were no febrile seizures represented in this node of the tree:

Hospital & ~motrin & ~area & ~itch, seizure & ~motrin or

seizure & ~ motrin & hospital

The second part of the rule that follows the "OR" condition is the most economical and states that if the words "hospital" and "seizure" appear and it is not "motrin" related, then the incident was marked as serious. The first rule also picked up cases where there were no "area" and "itch" words.

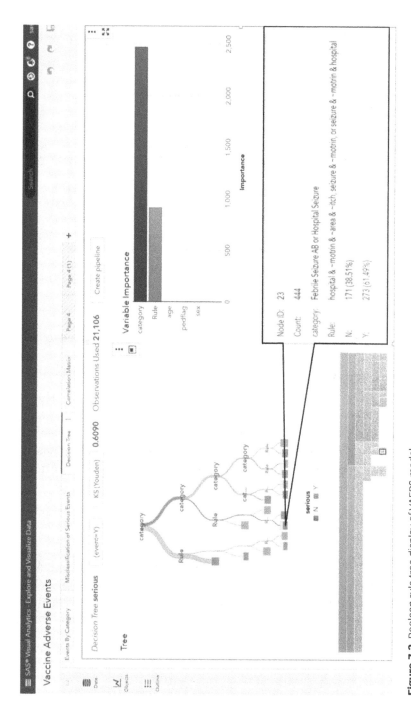

Figure 7.3 Boolean rule tree display of VAERS model.
Source: B. deVille.

SUMMARY

Boolean rules and text categories often outperform numeric data products in prediction and classification tasks. These text products also have interpretive benefits, since the rules and categories are expressed in natural language terms. The Boollear rules engine employs a g-test that is used as an information gain metric to calibrate inclusion of terms in the construction of the Boolean rule and also as a significance test to ensure the validity of rules that are constructed. The divide-and-conquer characteristics of Boollear equip it to identify narrow subregions of data, often with rare targets, that may easily be overlooked by more traditional linear models.

NOTES

i. J. Cox and Z. Zhao, "System for Efficiently Generating k-Maximally Predictive Association Rules with a Given Consequent," US Patent Number 20140337271 (2014).

ii. Z. Zhao, J. Cox, R. Albright, and N. Jin, "Using Boolean Rule Extraction for Taxonomic Text Categorization for Big Data," *Proceedings of the SAS® Global Forum 2015 Conference* (Cary, NC: SAS Institute Inc., 2015). https://support.sas.com/resources/papers/proceedings15/.

iii. SAS Institute Inc. SAS® Text Miner 14.1: High-Performance Procedures (Cary, NC: SAS Institute Inc., 2015).

iv. R.R. Soka, and F.J. Rohlf, *Biometry: The Principles and Practice of Statistics in Biological Research* (New York: W. H. Freeman, 1994).

v. Zhao et al. "Using Boolean Rule Extraction for Taxonomic Text Categorization for Big Data."

vi. Vaccine Adverse Event Reporting System (VAERS), https://vaers.hhs.gov/about.html. Published by the Centers for Disease Control and Prevention (CDC), and the Food and Drug Administration (FDA), agencies of the US Department of Health and Human Services (HHS). Date of Access: 12/1/2020.

CHAPTER **8**

Speech to Text

INTRODUCTION

Researchers have noted that audio files can be preprocessed into an unstructured data stream that can then be used in much the same way as a regular text corpus for analytic processing.[i] There is a large market potential and consequently a growing demand for solutions in this area. To illustrate the speech-to-text-to-analytics process, we present a case study that processes consumer audio feedback.

PROCESSING AUDIO FEEDBACK

While it has become easier for consumers to provide feedback to the producer in various forms, one problem for businesses occurs where there is no further information present about the provider of the feedback. Since the provider may not login to a portal or online platform – where fields like name, age, sex are included – businesses may not have access to this information. In this example, we discuss how audio analytics can be used to derive and establish a persona around the feedback provider by predicting sex, age group, ethnicity, and other categorical information. Not only will this help businesses in understanding the demographics of the providers of the feedback but will also help correlate this information to the comments received. The end product will help businesses craft better, more fine-tuned strategies.

Although this approach is relevant in extracting information from textural data in general, in this use case, we are going to explore methods that enable us to extract information from audio data. We are going to illustrate the process of how Mel Frequency Cepstral Coefficients (MFCC), as described in Jain and Harris,[ii] and acoustic features can be extracted from any audio file, and how these features can be used to categorize or classify the source of the audio. The categorization we will focus on is aligned mostly with gender, age, and accent – that is, we will be using these MFCC and acoustic features to predict whether the voice from an audio clip carries information that can reveal male or female gender, the possible age group of the audio source, and the likely geographical accent. Additionally, we are going to strengthen the information derived with respect to the persona with the associated sentiment and latent conversational topic prediction.

Business Problem

Almost all consumer-based businesses today have a feedback system that captures the viewpoint of the entity who is using the service or product. Although much of this feedback exists in the form of text, there are many advantages to including audio feedback, since it is often easier from the customer's point of view to provide spoken feedback rather than written forms. Currently, there are several virtual assistants, such as Siri, Cortana, Alexa, and Google Assistant. These environments have become test beds for the construction of audio and speech synthesis approaches that have migrated to other solutions in a variety of customer-centric areas – for example, facilitating product search.

Process Components

Audio (Speech) Processing

- **Preprocessing speech.** The initial phase in any automated audio/speech analytics problem normally consists of extracting features from audio signal input that enable the machine-learning algorithms to distinguish between useful acoustic content and less useful portions and signal impurities. A popular approach involves the computation of MFCCs.
- **Speech feature engineering.** The primary feature of human speech is that the sound waves that human beings generate are transformed in line with the form and structure of the vocal tract. The vocal tract is responsible for determining what sound ultimately gets transmitted and perceived. If we think of the underlying problem as estimating this form and structure, then the problem resolves to providing a correct depiction of the *phoneme* that is being sent and received. The form and structure of the vocal tract creates a sound that can be captured and described as an audio sample plot, as shown in Figure 8.2. The audio sample

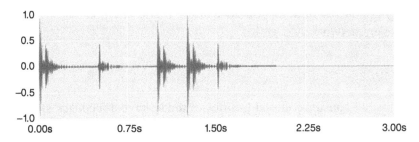

Figure 8.1 Audio sample plot (amplitude vs. time).
Source: G. Singh Bawa.

can be viewed as a function of *spectral density* that consists of various frequencies and amplitudes. Figure 8.1 illustrates the signal frequency shown on the horizontal axis and the associated amplitude, shown on the vertical axis. These densities form an envelope that can be algorithmically manipulated.

MFCCs are one of the most widely used features for speech recognition exercises, first proposed by Davis and Mermelstein.[iii] Before the introduction of MFCCs, linear prediction coefficients (LPCs)[iv] and linear prediction cepstral coefficients (LPCCs)[v] were the most commonly used approaches in this domain. These later approaches were extensions of hidden Markov model (HMM) classifiers.[vi]

The generated audio signal is continuously fluctuating; however, for simplification, let us initially assume that for shorter time scales, the signal does not alter in a statistically significant manner. For this reason, we will divide the signal into 20–40 ms frames. Frames shorter than this will not produce a sufficiently robust sample to obtain a consistent spectral estimate. In the case of a longer interval, there is a possibility of the signal changing across the frame a little more than expected.

The next step involves calculating the frame-specific power spectrum. The motivation behind this comes from our understanding of the receiving part of human-to-human speech – the cochlea in the human ear. The cochlea experiences vibration at different areas on its surface based on the frequencies of the sound coming in. The brain understands the different frequencies of sound waves received based on the vibrations that have been registered on the surface of the cochlea. The underlying nerve endings send signals to the brain,

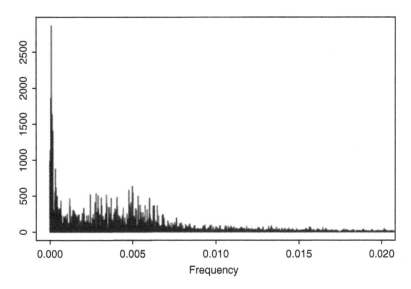

Figure 8.2 Periodogram using Fast Fourier Transforms (FFTs).
Source: G. Singh Bawa.

basically transcribing the received signal into a neural pattern. In this way, the cochlea acts as a periodogram for human beings and addresses the critical function of identifying the different frequencies that are present within a frame.

The estimates from the power spectrum of the periodogram also contain a substantial amount of information that does not hold much value for purposes of speech to text processing. The human periodogram of the cochlea does not have the ability to differentiate between frequencies that are very closely spaced. This phenomenon becomes much more noticeable with an increase in the number and frequencies in the frame. To deal with this increase in complexity, we can take bands within the periodogram and add them up to give a summary of the amount of energy existing in the different frequency bands. This leads to the idea of having the Mel Filterbank. In Figure 8.3 we see that the width of the bands in the Mel Filterbank keeps increasing toward the right – here, the first filter band is extremely restricted. This indicates the existence of the amount of energy near to the frequency value of 0 Hertz. This is because most variations in frequencies are generally captured in low-frequency ranges. With frequencies increasing, the Mel filters start getting broader since the concern about

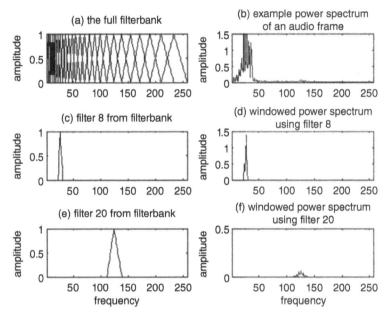

Figure 8.3 Illustrative functionality of Mel Filterbank.
Source: G. Singh Bawa.

variations decreases with increasing frequency. The interest then lies simply on the amount of energy existing at each of the bands. The Mel scale helps in providing guidance on spacing the filter banks and how broad the width should be.

Once the filter bank specific energies are obtained, a logarithmic transformation is made. Once again, the motivation behind this mirrors the hearing ability of human beings. The primary rationale is that human beings do not hear loudness on a linear scale. Studies have shown that to have a perception of almost double the volume of sound, the energy required is approximately eight times. This translates into the fact that if the sound is inherently loud, then it would not sound much different even if there are huge variations in energy. Thus, a compression operation such as the logarithmic transformation brings the features much more in line with how auditory signals affect the human ear. The reason for using a logarithmic transformation instead of any polynomial transformation is to facilitate the use of cepstral mean subtraction, a channel normalization technique.

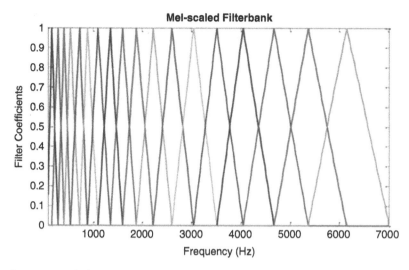

Figure 8.4 Mel Filterbank showing overlapping frequency patterns.
Source: G. Singh Bawa.

The last step involves the computation of the discrete cosine transformation (DCT) of the logarithm of the filter bank energies. The rationale for using a DCT is twofold: (1) As shown in Figure 8.4, the way that the Mel Filterbanks are created results in overlapping frequency patterns; and (2) because of this, the resulting energies show reasonably high correlations among each other. The DCT transformation helps in decorrelating the energies, thereby allowing the corresponding diagonal covariance matrices to be useful in modeling the features, for example, with a hidden Markov model classifier.

It should be noted that only 12 of the 26 coefficients from the DCT are retained and are actually useful. The reason behind doing so is that the higher coefficients denote faster variations in the filter bank energies (which means minimal improvement would be achieved by keeping them).

Feature Engineering

Feature engineering is the process of extracting features from the pre-processed input signal that can be used to construct the components of the typical predictive and classification models we use in various

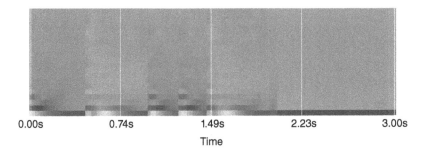

0.00s   0.74s   1.49s   2.23s   3.00s

Time

Figure 8.5 MFCC features vs. time (without scaling).
Source: G. Singh Bawa.

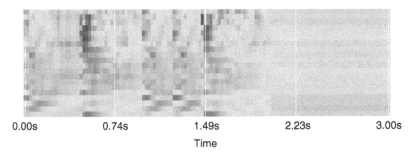

0.00s   0.74s   1.49s   2.23s   3.00s

Time

Figure 8.6 MFCC features vs. time (scaled).
Source: G. Singh Bawa.

analytic tasks. One method, described here, relies on studies of the acoustic interaction between animals. These studies have provided useful background in the form of behavioral studies and evolution theories.[vii] The studies depend heavily on the quantification of the acoustic signal structures and the resulting assessment of behavior context. Because these methods to measure and compare the structural form of signals have been important in the study of animal behavior, they provide a useful test bed that can be extended to more general applications.

As an example of this step, we will use characteristic products from an open-source R package to illustrate the estimation of the acoustic features contained in our data (the consumer audio and speech content). The package *warbleR* illustrates the study of signal structures of acoustic data originating from animals. Additionally, the package enables users to input their own audio content into the workflow, thereby facilitating spectrographic visualization and estimation of acoustic parameters.

The acoustic parameters we will be testing in our model are created by the *Specan* function in the *warbleR* package. The individual features that are created are as follows:

- **meanfreq:** amplitude-weighted mean of frequency within provided frequency band-pass filter
- **sd:** frequency standard deviation
- **freq.median:** that particular frequency where the signal is partitioned into two portions having identical energy
- **freq.Q25 and freq.Q75:** first and third quartile frequency – same as above, but divides the signal into 25–75 splits
- **freq.IQR:** interquartile frequency range
- **time.median:** median time that partitions the signal in two portions of equal energy
- **time.Q25 and time.Q75:** first and third quartile time – same as above, but divides the signal into 25–75 splits
- **time.IQR:** interquartile time range
- **skew:** asymmetry metric of the spectrum
- **kurt:** how peaked the spectrum looks
- **sp.ent:** spectral entropy, or the distribution of the energy on frequency spectrum
- **time.ent:** time entropy, or the distribution of energy on the time envelope
- **entropy:** spectrographic entropy, or the combination (product value) of both time and spectral entropy
- **sfm:** spectral flatness
- **meanfun, minfun, and maxfun:** average, minimum, and maximum fundamental frequency measured across the acoustic signal
- **meandom, mindom, and maxdom:** average, maximum, and minimum of dominant frequency measured across the acoustic signal

- **dfrange:** range of the dominant frequency
- **modindx:** modulation index, the collective absolute difference between adjacent estimates of dominant frequencies, divided by range of dominant frequency
- **startdom, enddom:** dominant frequency estimate at the start and end of the signal
- **dfslope:** rate of change of the dominant frequency over time

Audio Classification

Audio classification exercises involve three separate phases: signal pre-processing, feature engineering, and classification. The first phase performs some preprocessing on the signals and splits the input signal into separate segments (which are then utilized for the second phase of engineering the associated features). This phase of feature extraction is necessary since it helps in reducing the dimensionality of data and characterizes the unstructured and complex data by vectorizing it. We have already discussed the first and second phase; in this section, we will talk about the third phase, where the audio data is finally classified.

As shown in Figure 8.5, the spectrogram that is produced from the sound signal is infrequent. We can manipulate the features as shown in Figure 8.6 to provide a more robust input signal in the predictors of our model. This means that the intensity of the noise is found in the lower area, and components that are strong are in higher areas of the associated spectrogram. Features such as the MFCC and the acoustic features, which can be derived from the spectrogram, are used by several machine-learning models to classify audio input. The classification model was constructed using a Random Forest classifier, an MLP (Multi-layer Perceptron model) and a Convolutional Neural Network model (CNN).

We extracted 45 features to use in the classification task. We kept 20 MFCC coefficients. The remaining 25 features are acoustic coefficients derived using the Specan function in R. It should be noted that the first MFCC coefficient, or the 0th feature, adds the equivalent of a constant value to the audio spectrum model. The common practice is to use the first 13 features while ignoring the 0th one. In our model, we kept the first as it is and have taken the first 20 MFCC coefficients in our feature vector.

The data set that we have used is the common voice speech corpus data set, which consists of speech data that have been read by users of the website in addition to different text snippets from blogs, movies, and other publicly available speech corpora. In addition to the audio content, the data set consists of the age group of the narrator, if reported – for example, teens, twenties, and so on – the gender of the narrator, and the accent (such as US, Australia, Filipino).

Ideally, the MLP model is a feedforward artificial neural network with three node layers – input, hidden, and output. This architecture is diagrammed in Figure 8.7. The MPL model uses a supervised learning procedure known as backpropagation for training. Here, we implemented the MLPClassifier that comes in the *Scikit-learn* package in Python. We used the *Stochastic Gradient Descent* solver, which does parameter updates using the gradient of the loss function against the

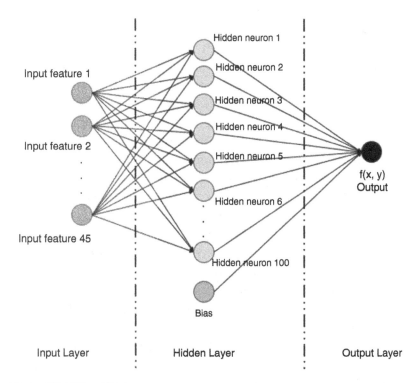

Figure 8.7 MLP architecture.
Source: G. Singh Bawa.

parameter that is currently being updated. An alpha parameter of value 0.0001 was used for L2 regularization. This helps in preventing overfitting by applying a penalty on high scale weights.

The Random Forest classifier was also used from the *scikit-learn* package in Python. The number of trees in the forest was set to 1000. The Gini function was used to measure the quality of split. The remaining parameters were kept at the default settings.

The architecture of the CNN model is illustrated in Figure 8.8. For the CNN implementation, we used the sequential approach from the *Keras* package in Python. This approach is easy to implement and removes any dependency on the functional API. *Keras* effectively has either the "sequential" or the "modular" framework. The sequential method is much simpler to implement, as layers can easily be stacked consecutively using the model.add() function. The architecture of the CNN model generally employs a convolutional layer, followed by a pooling layer. These are normally stacked over time (when the input space is quite large the time frames are pooled to minimize complexity). In our case, we are using a smaller frame of data so we will only pool once so as to preserve the information in the data space as much as possible. Our focus will be on building out more features using convolution so that we can learn more features to use in the classification. The approach is similar to building the contours that are observed in the MFCCs. The final product involves pooling it down and flattening it out to build a number of dense, fully connected layers.

We first start off the Conv2D layer with the 45 features having a 3×3 convolution and use a ReLU (Rectified Linear Unit) function. The stride parameter used is 1×1 since the input space is essentially small. In case the input space was high, the stride can be made 2×2 with the first kernel convolution being a 5×5; this way the number of parameters that we are solving for can be kept manageable. The padding parameter can be either "valid" or "same." "Valid" does not preserve the dimensions of the input matrix – hence we are going with "same." We add in totality four convolution layers – the more the layers, the better the learning. The filters used is increased in powers of 2: 16, 32, 64, 128 – the idea is to get more specific as the data starts to convolute down each layer. Once the convolution layers are done, we do the maxpooling with a 2×2 kernel MaxPool2D.

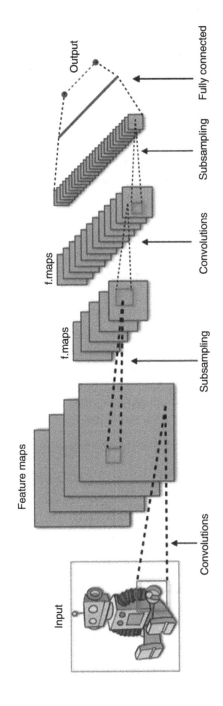

Figure 8.8 Typical CNN architecture.
Source: Aphex34, Retrieved from: https://commons.wikimedia.org/w/index.php?curid=45679374. Licensed under CC-BY-SA-4.0.

We then add a dropout of 0.5 just before we start flattening. Once it is flattened, we add the fully connected dense layers starting from 128 filters and gradually decreasing by powers of 2 with the final dense layer having filters with the count of categories to be predicted. In the final dense layer, since we are using categorical cross-entropy, the activation function is kept "softmax." In the model.compile() step, we use the loss function as categorical cross-entropy and optimizer as "adam."

From our experiment we observed that there is a substantial increase in accuracy of the model on the test data set while using acoustic features along with MFCC features compared to using MFCC only. Figure 8.9 shows the input variables for the Random Forest, ranked in order of importance. Also, in terms of classifier, the Random Forest classifier was comparatively better than the MLP classifier. However, as shown in Table 8.1 the Convolutional Neural Network architecture provided the best results.

Thus, we use the CNN classifier to make predictions on the audio content data for gender, age group, and accent. These predictions help us get a fair idea of the persona of the feedback provider.

In Table 8.1, we see the variable importance for both MFCC features and acoustic features. The fact that the first quartile of time and spectral flatness are the most important features demonstrate the explanatory power of acoustic features in predicting the gender of the audio source.

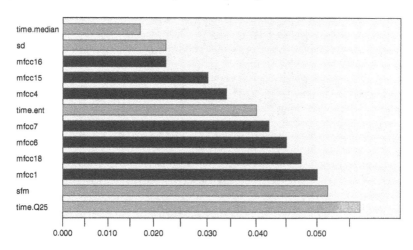

Figure 8.9 Variable importance (from Random Forest).
Source: G. Singh Bawa.

Table 8.1 Improvement in Accuracy Across Methods for Gender Classification

Model	MFCC only	MFCC + Other Acoustic Features
MLP	0.32	0.34
Random Forest	0.39	0.51
CNN	0.43	0.64

FURTHER ANALYSIS: SENTIMENT AND LATENT TOPICS

Apart from the categorical predictions made on the audio content that develops a rough persona of the feedback providers' demographics, further analysis can be made on the audio content. As illustrated in Figure 8.10, the audio feedback is converted to text, several text analytics models can be implemented and executed on the textual content.

In this case, since the audio data is consumer feedback, we focus primarily on extracting the associated sentiment of the feedback and try to extract the latent topic of the discussion for the feedback received. Ideally, these two text analytics models help understand consumers sentiment behind the feedback – whether it was a positive or negative or neutral sentiment – and what the most probable latent topic might be in the feedback that was provided. If there is a requirement of deeper sentiment estimation, we can also perform a mood-state prediction (mood state is a more general emotional predisposition compared to sentiment which is typically expressed toward a specific target).

To establish the associated sentiment and mood state, we use the NRC lexicon;[viii] this consists of slightly more than 14,000 tokens and their association to the eight basic emotions and mood states – anger, anticipation, disgust, fear, joy, sadness, surprise, and trust – as well as a high-level positive–negative association. A pretrained model specific to the domain in question, using similar data sets, can be useful in identifying what the latent topics generally speak about. Topic modeling techniques such as SAS topic modeling or general approaches like LSA and LDA will help establish the latent topics present within the training data; for example, service, product, pricing, ambience,

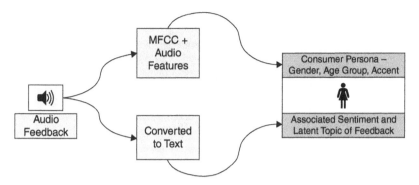

Figure 8.10 Process flow of generating value from audio feedback.
Source: G. Singh Bawa.

cleanliness. Once new feedback is received, predictions can be made to identify the document-topic associations so that the most likely topic can be identified. Thus, apart from establishing the persona of the consumer who provided the audio feedback, we can also generate other pieces of information such as the associated sentiment and topic by converting the audio content to text.

CONCLUSION

Data science and number crunching has become a baseline activity with every organization in any domain of business. Initial efforts involving the analysis of simple and structured numerical data have moved on to development of complex new technologies and algorithms to tackle the increasing scope and availability of unstructured data. The idea and practice of extracting knowledge from unstructured data has been growing exponentially. The amount of data and growth of data are almost unquantifiable and certainly beyond the grasp of normal comprehension.

This unstructured data available today assumes different forms such as text, image, video, audio clip, sensor data, IOT data, and much more – the list of data sources is close to inexhaustible. Any data not present in a regularized form on which algorithms can be applied easily belongs to this huge sea of unstructured data. In this use case, our focus was specifically on capturing and extracting information from audio data. We have discussed the associated methods and approaches that can help businesses to extract information from audio data and use it for fine-tuning their strategies accordingly.

What started off as just a simple piece of audio content is now enabling us to understand not only the sentiment, mood state, and latent topic but also the demographic features of the consumer such as gender, age group, and even the geographical accent of speech. Eventually, the insights generated from the audio content will help in more effective strategies for business organizations.

NOTES

i. Belamarić Wilsey, Biljana and Xiaozhuo Cheng (2020). *Sound Insights: A Pipeline for Information Extraction from Audio Files. SAS Global Forum* (Cary, NC SAS Institute Inc., 2020). https://www.sas.com/content/dam/SAS/support/en/sas-global-forum-proceedings/2020/4434-2020.pdf

ii. A. Jain and H. Harris, *Speaker Identification using MFCC and HMM Based Techniques* (Gainesville: University of Florida, 2004).

iii. S.B. Davis and P. Mermelstein, *Comparison of Parametric Representation for Monosyllabic Word Recognition in Continuously Spoken Sentences* (IEEE Trans. ASSP, Aug. 1980).

iv. S. Paulikas and R. Karpavičius, "Application of Linear Prediction Coefficients Interpolation in Speech Signal Coding," *Electronics and Electrical Engineering* 80 (2007): 39–42.

v. E. Wong and S. Sridharan, "Comparison of Linear Prediction Cepstrum Coefficients and Mel-Frequency Cepstrum Coefficients for Language Identification," *Proceedings of 2001 International Symposium on Intelligent Multimedia, Video and Speech Processing.* IEEE Cat. No.01EX489 (Hong Kong, China: ISIMP, 2001), 95–98.

vi. K. Lee and M. Slaney, "Automatic Chord Recognition from Audio Using a HMM with Supervised Learning," IEEE Transactions on Audio, Speech, and Language Processing 16, no. 2 (February 2008): 133–137; Daniel Jurafsky and J.H. Martin, *Speech and Language Processing* (Upper Saddle River, NJ: Pearson Prentice Hall, 2019).

vii. J.W. Bradbury and S.L. Vehrencamp, *Principles of Animal Communication* (Oxford: Sinauer Associates, Inc., Oxford University Press, 2011).

viii. S. Mohammad and P. Turney, "NRC Emotion Lexicon," *NRC Technical Report* (Ottawa, Canada: December 2013).

APPENDIX **A**

Mood State Identification in Text

ORIGINS OF MOOD STATE IDENTIFICATION

Mood state attribution belongs to a class of text analytics solutions that infer author attributes from text fragments taken from writings of a given user. The use of text analytics by biblical scholars to compare, contrast, and attribute authorship to various biblical passages is a long-standing example of this kind of application. In Chapter 4, *Document Content and Characterization*, we showed how work by Pennebaker was adapted to inferring the gender of a writer. Pennebaker, among others, also uses text analytics approaches to infer psychological characteristics of text authors.

Assessing user sentiment is an important capability, especially for buyer satisfaction ratings, primarily related to product sales and purchases. In addition to assessing the sentiment of a given document there have also been developments to determine the mood of a given document. Sentiment and mood have various meanings both in general discourse and in psychological assessment. Sentiment is a more specific assessment that tends to be oriented towards a given object and brand and is most usually positive, negative, or neutral. Mood, on the other hand, is a more general characterization of the author's general tone or disposition and the gradation of mood is more general and crosses various dimensions.

Mood state analytics evolved in the field of psychological research and psychometrics and has been adapted to use in the analysis of online sources, primarily social media. The application of mood state in psychological research was promoted by McNair et al. (1971)[i] in the creation of a Profile of Mood States (POMS) that consisted of responses to 65 adjectives that are rated by subjects on a 5-point scale. Six factors were derived from these responses:

1. tension-anxiety
2. depression-dejection
3. anger-hostility
4. fatigue-inertia
5. vigor-activity
6. confusion-bewilderment

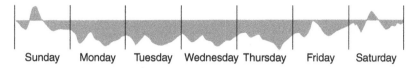

| Sunday | Monday | Tuesday | Wednesday | Thursday | Friday | Saturday |

Figure A.1 Social media monitoring mood through week.
Source: B. deVille

The POMS framework was updated (Heuchert and McNair, 2012)[ii] to include the addition of a new dimension, labeled "Friendliness."

One of the earliest adaptations of the POMS framework to internet activity was by Bollen et al. (2011a).[iii] Bollen's team adapted POMS to web-based conversations to form six dimensions of mood with minimally revised labels: tension, depression, anger, vigor, fatigue, confusion. Bollen used the extended Mood State profile to predict several outcomes such as mood shifts in Twitter conversations throughout the day, weekly variations in mood and geographic differences. Later, Bollen examined the relationship between mood state in social media and stock market outcomes (Bollen et. al. 2011b).[iv] Figure A.1 provides an illustration of some of the observations: here we can see elevated mood on the weekend, and generally better moods on Monday and Friday.

Other analysts were interested in determining whether the overall mood within social media sites is relatively positive or negative, and then to predict various outcomes such as book sales (Gruhl, Guha, Kumar, Novak, Tomkins, 2005),[v] box office receipts (Mishne and Glance, 2006),[vi] and success in blogs devoted to weight loss (Chung, Jones, Liu, & Pennebaker, 2008).[vii]

An Approach to Mood State Developed at SAS

A team of researchers at SAS Institute began adapting the emerging work on Mood States as applied to internet communications. This resulted in the development of a process that was documented and submitted for patent protection under the US Patent and Trademark Office. A Patent for Mood State Determination was awarded to Lehman et al. (2015).[viii] The previous work by Bollen et al. (2011b) in using mood state to predict outcomes in the public mood and stock market outcomes is cited in the patent filing. Other sources cited in the patent include Kennedy, et al. (2006),[ix] Watson et al. (1999),[x] Snyder and Barzilay (2007),[xi] and Bermingham et al. (2010).[xii]

Background and Discussion

Lehman et al. (2015)[xiii] note various use cases for the applicability of internet or communication media on mood state determination including blog entries, tweets, posts on social networking websites, online conversations, and newspaper articles. They also note the applicability for various purposes including marketing, customer relationship management, and political and brand analysis.

There is a discussion in the patent filing that draws a distinction between mood state and sentiments analysis. In sentiment analysis, the document may indicate a positive sentiment, a negative sentiment, or a neutral sentiment. Documents typically do not contain degree of sentiment, for example, highly positive or extremely negative. Typically, background emotions such as depression, fear, or anger are not recorded. The patent filing also notes that the linguistic rules to derive sentiment are complex, project-specific, and time consuming. Several benefits of mood state metrics are noted:

- The metrics are repeatable: a generic mood taxonomy is available for all industries.
- There is potential for real-time conversation monitoring.
- Greater dimensionality and richer data enhance predictions in analytic models.
- 12 mood scores are created rather than a simple sum of binary positive/negative sentiment.
- More precision is available since within each of the 12 moods, a scale of 1–3 to measure the intensity of the mood is constructed.
- The method is more generally available and more generally applicable.

The filing concludes by noting the desirability of mood state indicators to provide more analytical variables, better analytical depth, and reusability over different industries and situations.

The Lehman et al. (2015)[xiv] patent filing follows the established practice from the psychometrically based POMS framework, as well as the emerging practice of applying mood state analytics to internet-based communication. They arranged mood states along six main dimensions with opposing positive and negative sub-metrics in each of the six dimensions, as shown in Table A.1.

Unique Features of the SAS Approach

Several features (or "claims") were established in the SAS patent for mood state that serve as the unique basis for the intellectual property:

1. It establishes a taxonomy to map text to one or more of the mood categories.

2. A dimensional weight for the text is established during the mapping so that the mood weight reflects intensity of the text–mood dimension association.

3. Text proximity modifiers can be identified in the text to adjust the mood weight up or down, depending on the modifier.

4. The modifiers may be dampers or amplifiers and may also switch the polarity of the text association so that positive matches become negative matches, and vice versa.

5. A process to accumulate the weight over the entire text is specified.

Table A.1 Mood State Dimensional Labels and Polar Composites

Dimensional Label	Positive Mood	Negative Mood
"Tension"	Composed (+)	Anxious (−)
"Depression"	Elated (+)	Depressed (−)
"Anger"	Agreeable (+)	Hostile (−)
"Vigor"	Confident (+)	Unsure (−)
"Fatigue"	Energetic (+)	Tired (−)
"Confusion"	Clearheaded (+)	Confused (−)

Modifiers and Polarity Switching

Lehman et al. (2015)[xv] note that linguistic and psychological studies show that there is more to a mood than just "positive" or "negative" feelings. They note that "ecstatic" can be signaled by *can't complain* or by words like *happy* or *thrilled*. Similarly, "depressed" can be signaled by *glum, sad,* and *devastated*. In the proposed weighting scheme, a word like *glum* might get a weight of 1, whereas *sad* would get a weight of 2 and *devastated* would get a weight of 3. If all three terms appeared in a text fragment, then the combined score for "depressed" in the text fragment would be 6.

An Example Mood State Process Flow

For purposes of our example, we will use a framework outlined in Figure A.2.

Figure A.2 shows there are six dimensions consisting of six paired indicators. Each paired indicator reflects underlying positive and negative aspects of the associated dimension.

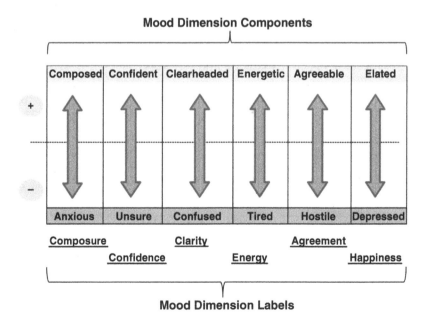

Figure A.2 Mood state dimensional components and polarity.
Source: B. deVille

The three main sub-processes in document mood state determination are summarized Figure A.3. They are:

1. Create taxonomy.

2. Populate mood dimensions.

3. Create standard mood state scores.

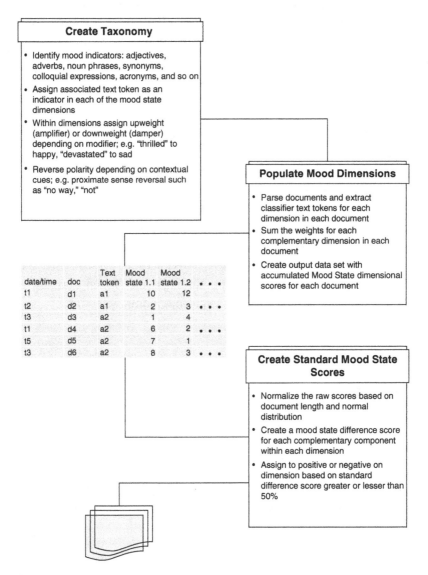

Figure A.3 Mood state score development process.
Source: B. deVille

These three sub-processes are briefly described and illustrated below.

Mood State Taxonomy: An Example Build

Both traditional psychometric researchers and internet-based text analysts have a similar challenge: how to infer psychological attributes based on semantic signifiers. There are now several internet-based resources available to assist in the construction of a taxonomy to populate the mood dimensions. One of the more general-purpose tools is the online thesaurus of the *Oxford English Dictionary* (1989).[xvi]

A search on the web can exploit an online thesaurus to find synonyms that can be used to map text fragments to dimensional scores. An example screen capture is shown in Figure A.4.

Table A.2 shows potential entries for the six positive dimensional states of *composed* through *elated*. The negative dimensions are not shown here.

Another useful resource is WordNet (G.A. Miller, R. Beckwith, C.D. Fellbaum, D. Gross, K. Miller. 1990).[xvii] WordNet is a database of English nouns, verbs, adjectives, and adverbs. These parts of speech are grouped into sets of cognitive synonyms called *synsets*. Each synset expresses a particular concept. Concepts are linked and can be browsed so that the end user can explore semantic relations.

Figure A.4 Example web search for mood state synonyms.
Source: B. deVille

Table A.2 Textual Indicators of Six Positive Mood States from Web Search

Composed	Confident	Clarity
calm	self-assured	lucidity
collected	assured	lucidness
cool	sure of oneself	clearness
and collected	self-confident	perspicuity
as cool as a cucumber	positive	intelligibility
coolheaded	assertive	comprehensibility
controlled	self-assertive	coherence
self-controlled	self-possessed	simplicity
serene	believing in oneself	plainness
tranquil	self-reliant	explicitness
relaxed		lack of ambiguity
at ease		precision
Energy	**Agreeable**	**Elated**
vitality	pleasant	contented
vigor	pleasing	content
life	enjoyable	cheerful
liveliness	pleasurable	cheery
animation	nice	merry
vivacity	to one's liking	joyful
spirit	appealing	jovial
spiritedness	engaging	jolly
fire	satisfying	joking
passion	fine	jocular
ardor	charming	gleeful
zeal	delightful	carefree
verve	likable	untroubled

Populate the Mood Dimensions

Once we have a taxonomy, then our next step is to parse the input document and identify word-terms that match the taxonomy entries. For each match, a score is set for the mood indicator in the document. In the process developed by Lehman et al. (2015), the score may be

Table A.3 Example Term Weight Adjustments

Word-term	Mood indicator	Term weight
Downcast	Depressed	1
Disagreeable	Hostile	2
Hurt	Depressed	1
Sobbing	Depressed	3

adjusted by either increasing the score, decreasing it, or potentially reversing its polarity.[xviii] An example is shown in Table A.3, where the terms *downcast, disagreeable, hurt,* and *sobbing* yield a "Depressed" mood indicator score of 5 and a "Hostile" mood indicator score of 2.

Figure A.5 provides an example text fragment to illustrate how to populate scores in several dimensional metrics. Here, *hope* is used to trigger a "confident" score; *working so hard* triggers an "energetic" score; *need to sleep* triggers a "tired" score; and *difficult problem* triggers an "unsure" score.

Generate Raw Mood State Scores

In our example, we show the results of a sample of documents from a larger collection that have been processed through a mood

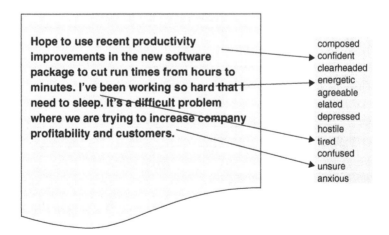

Figure A.5 Text and target metric mapping.
Source: B. deVille

Table A.4 Sample Document with Raw Mood State Scores

Doc ID	Doc length	composed	anxious	confident	unsure	clear	confused	energetic	tired	agreeable	hostile	elated	depressed
999	23								6				
3812	26			4									
22120	24			1						9		2	
32094	27	6		2									
48604	19	6									1	3	
100905	26				4								
110248	24			2							9		
117372	23		5				2						
123997	23							13				23	
126405	25			14									
126830	24				4								

state taxonomy. Example mood state scores, constructed for purposes of illustration, are shown in Table A.4.

Table A.4 displays the 11 example documents with Doc ID's ranging from 999 to 126,830. For each document, a "Doc length" field is shown. This expresses the length of the source document as a raw count of the number of words. The raw scores for various mood state components ranging from "composed" to "depressed" have been constructed for this example data set.

Adjust Mood State Scores

Because the raw scores were produced from documents of different lengths, it is possible for a document to get a larger score because it has more words in the document than other documents that have fewer words. A simple adjustment to enable us to compare the scores from all documents in the collection is to divide the score by the document length. We show this result in Table A.5.

In Table A.5, we can see that the raw scores for "composed" in documents 32094 and 48604 have been adjusted for word length so that, while the raw scores were the same, the adjusted scores

Table A.5 Mood Score Adjusted by Document Word Length

Doc ID	Doc length	composed	anxious	confident	unsure	clearheaded	confused	energetic	tired	agreeable	hostile	elated	depressed
999	23								0.26				
3812	26			0.15									
22120	24		0.04							0.38		0.08	
32094	27	0.22		0.07									
48604	19	0.32										0.05	0.16
100905	26			0.15									
110248	24			0.08						0.38			
117372	23		0.22				0.09						
123997	23							0.57				1.00	
126405	25			0.56									
126830	24				0.17								

are different. This reflects the differing document lengths of 27 and 19, respectively.

Standardize the Mood State Scores

Standard scores have a mean of zero and a standard deviation of 1. In this example, we are going to transform the adjusted mood state scores to a standard score. This will allow us to manipulate the 12 positive and negative polarity components of each of the six-dimensional mood states. The standard score is computed by subtracting the raw adjusted score from the population mean and dividing the result by the standard deviation of the population score. Table A.6 shows the population mean and standard deviation that have been calculated for each of the 12 polarity dimensions in our example.

Table A.7 shows the computed standardized scores for the adjusted mood state dimensional entries. Each adjusted score has been standardized by subtracting the population mean and dividing by the standard deviation.

Table A.6 Mean and Standard Deviation Measures for the Mood State Dimensional Scale Entries

(mean, standard deviation)	composed	confident	clearheaded	energetic	agreeable	elated	depressed	hostile	tired	confused	unsure	anxious
μ	0.11	0.10	0.11	0.11	0.08	0.14	0.08	0.09	0.10	0.10	0.07	0.12
σ	0.04	0.05	0.05	0.06	0.06	0.09	0.04	0.06	0.06	0.04	0.04	0.05

Table A.7 Standardized Scores for the Dimensional Mood States

Doc ID	composed	anxious	confident	unsure	clearheaded	confused	energetic	tired	agreeable	hostile	elated	depressed
999							2.28					
3812			1.97									
22120		−1.2							4.9		−0.7	
32094	2.8		−0.5									
48604	5.5									−0.6	0.15	
100905			1.97									
110248			-0.3							4.45		
117372		1.72				−0.5						
123997							6.98				9.31	
126405			9.37									
126830				2.28								

As an example of the calculation, we can look at the standardized score of 2.8 in document 32,094 in the "composed" column of Table A.7. We can see that the score of 2.8 is the result of subtracting the adjusted score of 0.22 (shown in Table A.5) from the mean of 0.11

and dividing the result by the standard deviation of 0.04 (these are shown in Table A.6).

Map Scores into Range Buckets

In this step, we use the position of the standard score to compute whether it is 1, 2, or 3 standard deviations from the mean. We then convert the quantitative standard score into a small set of ordered buckets labeled 1, 2, or 3.

As an example, consider the score of 4.9 for the "agreeable" dimension, shown in Table A.7. When we calculate the standard deviation for this dimension, we get 0.43. The cutoffs for this dimension are shown in Table A.8.

The result of this transformation for the example data is shown in Table A.9. In the table header there is now an indicator of whether the column measures a positive aspect (+) or a negative aspect (−) of the underlying mood dimension.

Assign Overall Mood Score for the Documents

The overall mood score for the 12 consistent dimensions of the example data is shown in Table A.10. The scores are produced by forming an approximation of the averages of the bucket scores in the previous step. (Strictly speaking, the "average" of an ordered scale with three categories should be the mode, or most common value, so we are knowingly violating number theory with these calculations.)

Finally, we can compute the difference between the positive and negative dimensions to arrive at an overall mood score for each of the six major dimensions of mood. These results are shown in Table A.11.

Example Summary Mood State Characterization

In the example data considered here, the authors are composed and calm (score of 1 overall). They are not greatly confident in tone

Table A.8 Bucket Values and Standard Score Cutoffs for the "Agreeable" Dimension

Bucket Number	1	2	3
Standard Score cutoffs	<=−0.43	>−0.43 and <0.43	>=0.43

Table A.9 Dimensional Scores Mapped into Ordered Categories (Based on Standard Score)

Doc ID	Composed (+)	Anxious (−)	Confident (+)	Unsure (−)	Clearheaded (+)	Confused (−)	Energetic (+)	Tired (−)	Agreeable (+)	Hostile (−)	Elated (+)	Depressed (−)
999								3				
3812				3								
22120			2						3		2	
32094	3		2									
48604	3									2	2	
100905				3								
110248			2							3		
117372		2				2						
123997							3				3	
126405			3									
126830				3								

Table A.10 Overall Document Mood Score Based on Average Calculation Score

Composure		Confidence		Clarity		Energy		Agreement		Happiness	
composed (+)	anxious (−)	confident (+)	unsure (−)	clearheaded (+)	confused (−)	energetic (+)	tired (−)	agreeable (+)	hostile (−)	elated (+)	depressed (−)
3.00	2.00	2.25	3.00		2.00	3.00	3.00	3.00	2.50	2.33	

Table A.11 Overall Mood State for the Example Collection on Six Dimensions

Dimension	+	−	Overall
Composure	3.0	2.0	1
Confidence	2.3	3.0	−1
Clarity		2.0	−2
Energy	3.0	3.0	0
Agreement	3.0	2.5	1
Happiness	2.3		2

(score of –1). The language that is used is highly ambiguous and lacks precision (overall clarity score of –2). It seems that the positive and negative aspects of energy offset one another. The overall agreement is positive (1) and the general disposition is well above average in happiness (2).

NOTES

i. D.M. McNair, M. Lorr and L.F. Droppleman, *Manual for the Profile of Mood States (POMS)* (San Diego: Educational and Industrial Testing Service, 1971).

ii. J.P. Heuchert and D.M. McNair, *Profile of Mood States – Second Edition (POMS-2).* (Multi-Health Systems Inc., Toronto, 2012).

iii. J. Bollen, H. Mao and A. Pepe, "Modeling Public Mood and Emotion: Twitter Sentiment and Socio-Economic Phenomena." *Proceedings of the International AAAI Conference on Web and Social Media, 5(1),* 2011a. https://ojs.aaai.org/index.php/ICWSM/article/view/14171.

iv. J. Bollen, H. Mao and A. Pepe, "Twitter mood predicts the stock market," *Journal of Computational Science,* 2, 8, 2011b. http://singularityhub.com,m/20 10/1 0/21/twitter-predicts-the-stock-market/.

v. D. Gruhl, R. Guha, R. Kumar, J. Novak, and A. Tomkins, "The predictive power of online chatter," KDD '05: *Proceeding of the Eleventh ACM SIGKDD International Conference on Knowledge Discovery in Data Mining,* 78–87 (New York, NY, USA. ACM Press, 2005).

vi. G. Mishne and N. Glance, "Predicting movie sales from blogger sentiment," *AAAI 2006 Spring Symposium on Computational Approaches to Analysing Weblogs,* 2006.

vii. C.K. Chung, C. Jones, A. Liu, J.W. Pennebaker, "Predicting success and failure in weight loss blogs through natural language use," *Proc. of the 2nd International Conference on Weblogs and Social Media,* 2008 aaai.org.

viii. Thomas Lehman, Jody Porowski, Bruce Monroe Mills, Michael T. Brooks, and Heather Michelle Goodykoontz, "Computer-implemented systems and methods for mood state determination," United States patent US 9201866, issued December 1, 2015.

ix. Alistair Kennedy and Diana Inkpen, "Sentiment classification of movie reviews using contextual valence shifters," *Computational Intelligence* 22 (2) (2006): 110–125.

x. David Watson and Lee Anna Clark, "The PANAS-X: Manual for the positive and negative affect schedule-expanded form" (1999).

xi. Benjamin Snyder, and Regina Barzilay, "Multiple Aspect Ranking Using the Good Grief Algorithm," HLT-NAACL (2007).

xii. Adam Bermingham and Alan Smeaton, *Classifying Sentiment in Microblogs: Is Brevity an Advantage?* (Dublin City University: CLARITY: Centre for Sensor Web Technologies School of Computing, 2010).

xiii. Lehman et al., "Computer-implemented systems and methods for mood state determination."

xiv. Ibid.

xv. Ibid.

xvi. *Oxford English Dictionary*, 2nd ed. 20 vols. (Oxford: Oxford University Press, 1989). http://www.oed.com/.

xvii. G.A. Miller, R. Beckwith, C.D. Fellbaum, D. Gross, K. Miller, "WordNet: An Online Lexical Database," *Int. J. Lexicography*, 3 (4) (1990): 235–244.

xviii. Lehman et. al., "Computer-implemented systems and methods for mood state determination."

A Design Approach to Characterizing Users Based on Audio Interactions on a Conversational AI Platform

Online, interactive, intelligent personal agents (referred to as *bots*[i]) are now ubiquitous and accomplish a wide range of tasks that enhance the interface between human users and cloud-based computer services. Increasingly, these agents are built with artificial intelligence (AI) capabilities, and this expands their utility. The utility of these agents depends on their ability to correctly infer intentions and circumstances that characterize the user. In this use case, we outline a collection of processes and techniques to extract and quantify aspects of the sound and audio signal from audio interactions between user and the *bot* agent, to establish characteristics that lead to the attribution of end-user persona attributes such as gender, age, accent, and so on. Additionally, the audio signals are converted to a textual format and pretrained text analytics models are brought into the process to establish feature weights to infer latent intent from the interaction. This adds information to the interaction and thereby increases the accuracy and utility of the user-bot interaction.

AUDIO-BASED USER INTERACTION INFERENCE

A wide range of organizations is moving toward automation in conversational user interaction through the development of increasingly capable AI based audio user interaction bots and assistants. Historically, these AI assistants were text based; now voice-based assistants are becoming more prominent. Audio and voice-based systems are much faster and easier for the end-user than writing or typing. Although voice interaction has become easier for end-users, this creates issues for the AI assistant operators since, with voice-only information, there is typically no further information present about the end-user who is involved in the interaction. Voice-based systems do not typically require the user to log in to a portal or online platform where fields like name, age, and gender are typically collected during signup. The absence of portal-based user information means that potentially useful information such as user demographics are lost as context in the analysis of ensuing user interaction.

In this design, we have addressed this issue of how the audio signals from the end-users can be processed to infer and establish a persona around the end user. We create likelihood estimations to attribute end-user attributes of gender, age group, or dialect. This will help the bot platform managers to build out the demographic picture of the end-users and will also enhance the capabilities of incorporating the predicted information in the underlying conversation, ultimately helping to fine-tune conversational responses.

Recommendation Perspective vs. Conventional

Organizations that operate automated voice-based conversation platforms want to extract as much value as possible from their investments in this technology and so are motivated to engage in deeper levels of analysis of the audio data obtained from the conversations and interactions between the end-user and the AI bot. These analytics include:

- *Use audio data transcription and text analysis.* This process involves transcribing the speech/conversation between the bot and end-user to text. The resultant textual data is then passed through different layers of text analysis to identify key instances within the conversation, which reflects the end-user's interests, preferences, and expectations. The business's focus then shifts to mining the textual content with aim of improving customer experience, recommending cross-sell and up-sell opportunities, and minimizing customer loss propensities. Once the audio signal is converted to text there are fewer options left to identify or form a persona of the end-user. So, this approach misses out on the opportunity to mine fine-level detail that is contained in the audio signal itself.

- *Use audio data to establish the persona.* An alternative approach helps to bridge the gap between the raw audio speech signals and the typical text analytics. It focuses on utilizing the audio data to establish the persona of the end-user. Useful attributes such as likelihood of gender, age group, and geographical accent are mined from the audio signals before they are carried forward to the text analytical components. In this way, the platform operator obtains a unique acoustic signature of the end-user which can be later used to uniquely identify the end-user. The operator also infers end-user characteristics by predicting various persona attributes from the audio.

Sole Dependency on Text-Based Bots

Some platforms rely on exclusively on bots based on text interaction bots rather than audio-based bots. These text-based bots have a chat UI that requires an end-user sign on to converse with the bot. The sign-in option captures various fields of information about the end-user and helps the business in mining information for use in strategy development. The emergence of voice-based bots and the preference of end-users toward speaking to a bot rather than typing means that voice-based bots are becoming a preferable option in many situations. The conversation, user interaction, and information exchange in text-based bots tend to be more time-consuming and are often less preferred by end-users. The downside with the movement towards voice bots is less information on the end user. A switch to a voice bot could lead to a significant loss of information if the persona of the end-user and associated demographics is not available to the business.

We present here a solution to issues of information loss caused by switching from text-based to voice-based bots. The overall architecture of the solution is illustrated in Figure B.1. The solution

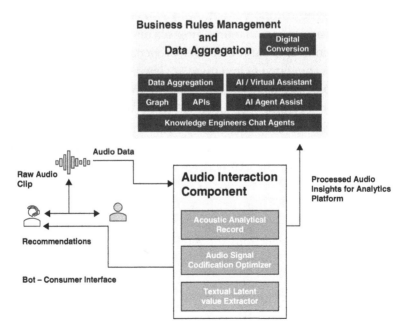

Figure B.1 Implementation scenario.
Source: G. Singh Bawa

helps to utilize the audio data from the voice interactions and establish a persona of the end-user by predicting different attributes such as gender, age group, and so on. Thus, businesses that are migrating towards voice-based bots from text-based bots can harness and mine information about the end-user to incorporate processing options that favor desirable end user interactions.

IMPLEMENTATION SCENARIO: VOICE-BASED CONVERSATIONAL AI PLATFORM

The overall architecture of a voice-based conversational artificial intelligence (AI) is described in Figure B.2. There are three main components: Acoustic Analytical Record, Audio Signal Codification Optimizer, and Textual Latent Value Extractor. These components are described below.

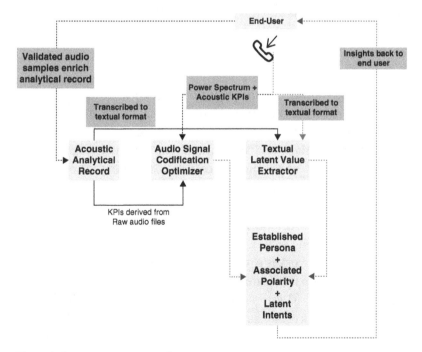

Figure B.2 Component process flow.
Source: G. Singh Bawa

Component Process Flow

Acoustic Analytical Record – Prerequisite

This component consists of labeled audio clips of human speech which contain one or more tags that match the required attributes for personas that the system will be configured to establish. When processed, each speech sample acts as entries for subsequent steps. The speech components require transformations that quantify the audio signal and configures it for machine processing. Acoustic and power spectrum processors that describes the audio signal effectively are required for this step. The form and structure of the speaker's vocal tract is the baseline template for the form of the short time power spectrum that is used in the pre-processing. The pre-processing is characterized by power spectrum coefficients. A few more additional acoustic features are also extracted based on audio signal frequency and amplitude. The analytical record is initially composed of speech samples and corresponding attribute tags and is subsequently converted to a quantifiable set of features—key performance indicators (KPIs)—that help describe the speech sample in an appropriate machine learning format.

Audio Signal Codification Optimizer

This component processes the quantifiable feature attributes (KPIs) from the acoustic analytical record. Audio signal codification involves three separate phases: (1) signal pre-processing, (2) feature engineering, and (3) likelihood estimation. The first two phases have been taken care of in the pre-processing component. The primary objective of the audio signal codification optimizer component is to optimize the codification process of any speech sample against the prospective persona attributes in the acoustic analytical record by estimating the likelihood scores for each tag. To do this, a feedforward artificial neural network is constructed for each persona attribute that receives the quantifiable features obtained from the previous component and optimizes its estimated weights across the different neural network layers. Once the stable optimized network is in place, any speech sample can be passed through the network by deconstructing it to the quantifiable KPI features. The feedforward neural network then estimates the likelihood for the available tags within the persona attribute and predicts the one with maximum likelihood.

Textual Latent Value Extractor

Apart from the codification exercise in the previous audio component, further value can be extracted from the speech samples. In this component, the speech samples are first converted to textual format and are then passed through a hybrid deep learning setup. This setup processes the textual content and extracts associated polarities from the interaction coupled with associated latent intents. To estimate the associated content-latent intent polarities a long short-term memory (LSTM) Neural Network is used. As implied by the name "long short-term memory," LSTM networks incorporate cyclic associations between the neural network layers, which are classically feed-forward layer-by-layer networks. This means that LSTM networks can incorporate sequence information between layers. In this setup, the token vector representations are first fed into a sentence-level LSTM neural network to capture sentence-level information. The output of the sentence-level process is merged with the target contextual vector and further fed into another bidirectional review-level LSTM resulting in the polarity probabilities. To establish user-interaction intentions, an extension is made of the word vector representations to model the latent probabilistic distribution of the collection of concurrent contextual tokens. The function of this step is to align to the extracted contextual intent to the user-interaction scenario.

Component 1: Acoustic Analytical Record – Prerequisite

This component is illustrated in Figure B.3. The main functionality consists of maintaining structured audio clips of human speech. Each record contains one or more tag fields that match persona attributes the system would be configured to establish. Audio clips consist of speech samples and therefore, once processed act as entry links to the next two components. The audio clips require transformation to quantify the audio signal of the speech sample and turn it into a digital record suitable for machine processing.

Plurality of Audio Samples

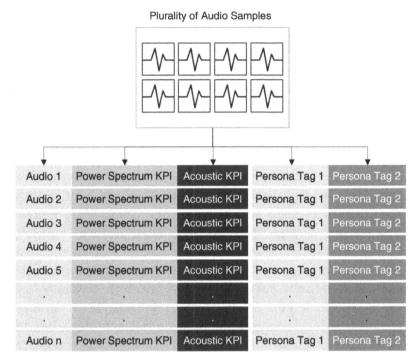

Figure B.3 Acoustic analytic record construction.
Source: G. Singh Bawa

The transformation requirements lead to the need of having acoustic and power spectrum KPI feature attributes that describes the audio signal effectively. The form and structure of the speaker's vocal tract serves as a model for the feature envelope for the short time power spectrum. This can be accurately depicted with the help of power spectrum coefficients.

Additional acoustic features may be extracted based on the audio signal frequency and amplitude. In this way, the analytical record and associated speech samples and corresponding attribute tags are converted into a quantifiable set of KPI features that describe the speech sample in a machine processing format.

New audio samples from future interactions are reinserted back into the audio record collection, based on feedback from the end user. If the prediction made by the proposed mechanism has a high-likelihood probability associated with it and is also acknowledged by end-user feedback, it can be reincorporated into the acoustic analytical record, thereby reinforcing and enriching the training dataset.

The generated audio signal fluctuates continuously. Based on the assumption that the signal does not alter in a statistically significant manner, the signal is divided into 20–40ms frames (a shorter interval will not produce sufficient samples required to obtain consistent spectral estimates). With longer intervals, there is a possibility of unmanageable the signal variability across the analysis frame.

Once the signals are divided into frames then the frame specific power spectrum is calculated using a periodogram. The estimates from the power spectrum of the periodogram contain a substantial amount of low-quality predictive information. Low-quality information accumulates with an increase in frequencies. High-quality bands of information in the periodogram identified and then added to reflect the amount of energy existing in different frequency bands. A separate scaling filter bank is used with diverging widths. The filter bank specific summed energies then are run through a logarithmic transformation to effectively normalize the various frequency bands.

As a final step a cosine transformation is applied to help de-correlate the overlapping energies that have been captured in the filter bank. The resulting coefficients then can be used as the signature for the specific audio signal.

Component 2: Audio Signal Codification Optimizer
This component is illustrated in Figure B.4. The main function is to process the quantifiable KPI feature attributes from the acoustic analytical record and estimates the likelihood of each of the tag fields by constructing one model for each persona attribute tag on the analytical record. Audio signal codification involves three separate phases:

1. Signal pre-processing
2. Feature engineering
3. Likelihood estimation

The first two phases have been taken care of in the initial component. The primary objective of the second component is to optimize the codification process of the speech samples for the prospective

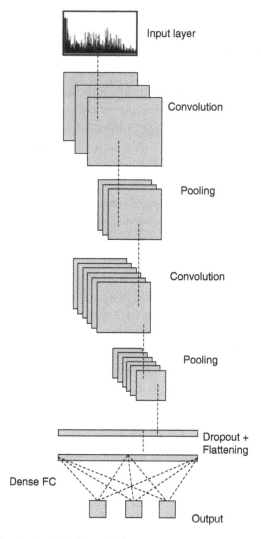

Figure B.4 Audio signal codification optimizer.
Source: G. Singh Bawa

persona attributes in the acoustic analytical record by estimating the likelihood scores for each tag.

Likelihood scores are estimated with a feedforward artificial neural network that is constructed for each persona attribute. The network receives the quantifiable features obtained from the previous component and optimizes the estimated weights across the different layers.

Once the stable optimized network is in place, any speech sample can be passed through the network by deconstructing it into its component quantifiable features.

The feedforward neural network will process any audio sample to estimate the likelihood for the available tags within the persona attribute and will produce a ranked list of available tags. This will identify the persona field with the maximum likelihood.

A Convolutional Neural Network model is constructed with the following architecture:

Convolution layer with kernel size 3×3

Max pooling layer with pool size 2×2

Convolution layer with kernel size 2×2

Max pooling layer with pool size 2×2

1 dropout layer and 1 flattening layer

2 dense layered neural network

Component 3: Textual Latent Value Extractor

Once the audio signal optimization has run, a further latent value extraction process can be applied. This component is illustrated in Figure B.5. Here, speech samples from the acoustic analytical record are first converted to a textual format. The text format is then passed through a hybrid deep-learning process that receives the textual content to extract associated polarities from the user interaction, together with associated latent intents.

To estimates polarities, an LSTM Neural Network is configured with an extension to include the associated contextual target. This process involves sub-tasks: the first is to set up a representation for a contextual target. Once possibility is contextual embedding, which is a form of vector representation. The second sub-task is to identify the primary context tokens for the specified target. For example, in the sentence "the screen of the phone is bigger, but the display is unclear," *bigger* is the contextual target for "screen" and *unclear* for "display."

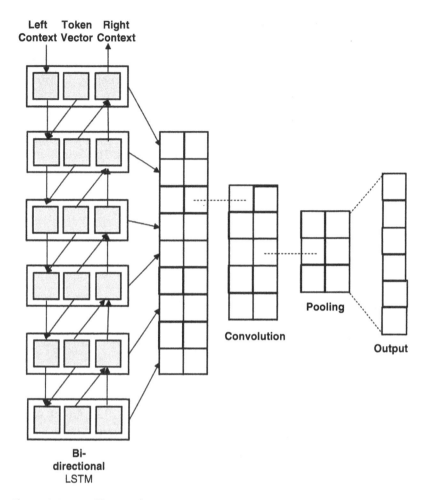

Figure B.5 Textual latent value extractor.
Source: G. Singh Bawa

A bidirectional LSTM neural network is used for context dependent polarity estimation since it captures the relations both within and between sentences. The solitary dependency on the sentences and their structures within the converted text is most useful since it takes care of all possible variations in the conversations.

The token vector representations are fed into a sentence-level bidirectional LSTM neural network. The output states of the network are merged with the target contextual vector and is further fed into another bidirectional summary-level LSTM to produce the polarity probabilities.

To establish the latent intents, an extension is made to the word vector representations. These word vectors are then added to the token concurrent probabilistic distributions. These enriched probability distributions enable the construction of models for the latent probabilistic distribution of collections of concurrent contextual tokens. This facilitates the alignment of these word fragments to the underlying intents in question.

Constructed Interaction

The constructed interaction of the various components are described in Figure B.6. The objective is to have a model that can learn dense word vectors jointly with the probabilistic latent interaction-level mixtures of latent intents.

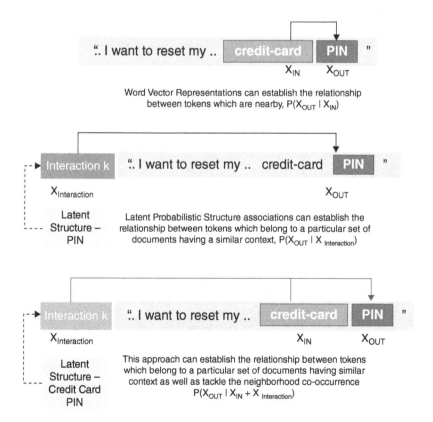

Figure B.6 Textual latent value extractor (detail).
Source: G. Singh Bawa

The result is to obtain the contribution of each of the underlying intents that are mapped on the interactions based on the granular token vector representations. For example, while a simple probabilistic latent intent model will be able to establish a latent intent as "Savings Account" based on the presence of tokens in the interaction such as "bank," "account," "savings," "balance," "pin," and so on, the modeling approach presented here extends the probabilistic intent model on top of the token vector representations. This leads to more complex vector representations of each of the underlying tokens to establish intents. For example, within "savings account," we might observe "savings account credential" (consisting of tokens like "savings," "account," "password," "PIN," and so on). Another example might include "savings account transactions" (consisting of tokens like "savings," "account," "balance," "loans," "credit," "debit," and so on).

NOTE

i. "Bots" are an emerging, generic term for autonomous computer network resident processes that interact with other processes and users operating using network resources.

SAS Patents in Text Analytics

Computer-Implemented System and Method for Text-Based Document Processing

This is foundational patent work that established the basis for treating textual products in a quantitative fashion to construct factorizations of documents (which would be later extended to produce text topics) as well as document clusters.

Patent number: 6996575

Abstract: A computer-implemented system and method for processing text-based documents. A frequency-of-terms data set is generated for the terms appearing in the documents. Singular value decomposition is performed upon the frequency of terms data set to form projections of the terms and documents into a reduced dimensional subspace. The projections are normalized, and the normalized projections are used to analyze the documents.

Type: Grant

Filed: May 31, 2002

Date of Patent: February 7, 2006

Assignee: SAS Institute Inc.

Inventors: James A. Cox, Oliver M. Dain

Method and System for Responding to User-Input Based on Semantic Evaluations of User-Provided Expressions

This is foundational patent work that extended the text parsing and semantic processing engine that SAS uses to break down incoming text into its part of speech components.

Patent number: 7809724

Abstract: A method for processing user input includes the step of receiving, during a session, via one of a plurality of media gateways, from a user, an expression having a semantic structure. The semantic structure of the expression is evaluated. An expression type is identified, responsive to the evaluation of the semantic structure. Based on the expression type, a response to the expression is generated. A determination is made as to whether to store the received expression, the response, and an identification of the user.

Type: Grant
Filed: January 12, 2007
Date of Patent: October 5, 2010
Assignee: SAS Institute Inc.
Inventors: Emmanuel Roche, Yves Schabes

Computer-Implemented Systems and Methods for Mood State Determination

This is an example of SAS patent work in assessing author attributes based on the types of expressions used and the semantic constructs that characterize the expressions.

Patent number: 9201866

Abstract: Computer-implemented systems and methods are provided for determining an overall mood score of a document. For example, the document is received from a computer-readable medium. A text segment in a document is identified to be indicative of a mood of the document. The text segment is mapped to a mood scale among a predetermined set of mood scales. A mood weight associated with the mood scale for the text segment is generated. An overall mood score of the document is determined based at least in part on the mood weight.

Type: Grant
Filed: January 8, 2015
Date of Patent: December 1, 2015
Assignee: SAS Institute Inc.
Inventors: Thomas Lehman, Jody Porowski, Bruce Monroe Mills, Michael T. Brooks, Heather Michelle Goodykoontz

Computer-Implemented Systems and Methods for Taxonomy Development

This patent shows how to create a classifier-based taxonomy based on establishing a distance-based metric to establish the precedence of classifiers with respect to the various levels of the taxonomy.

Patent number: 9116985

Abstract: Systems and methods are provided for generating a set of classifiers. A location is determined for each instance of a topic term in a collection of documents. One or more topic term phrases are identified, and one or more sentiment terms within each topic term phrase. Candidate classifiers are identified by parsing words in the one or more topic term phrases, and a colocation matrix is generated. A seed row of the colocation associated with a particular attribute is identified, and distance metrics are determined by comparing each row of the colocation matrix to the seed row. A set of classifiers are generated for the attribute, where classifiers in the set of classifiers are selected using the distance metrics.

Type: Grant

Filed: December 16, 2011

Date of Patent: August 25, 2015

Assignee: SAS Institute Inc.

Inventors: Bruce Monroe Mills, John Courtney Haws, John Clare Brocklebank, Thomas Robert Lehman

System for Efficiently Generating K-Maximally Predictive Association Rules with a Given Consequent

This patent is the basis for extracting association rules (rules joined by "AND" and "OR" expressions) as predictors of a given outcome in a text collection (such as topic or classification).

Patent number: 9117174

Abstract: This disclosure provides a computer-program product, system, method, and apparatus for accessing a representation of a category or item and accessing a set of multiple transactions. The transactions are processed to identify items found amongst the transactions, and the items are ordered based on an information-gain heuristic. A depth-first search for a group of best association rules is then conducted using a best-first heuristic and constraints that make the search efficient. The best rules found during the search can then be displayed to a user, along with accompanying statistics. The user can then select rules that appear to be most relevant, and further analytics can be applied to the selected rules to obtain further information about the information provided by these rules.

Type: Grant
Filed: July 21, 2014
Date of Patent: August 25, 2015
Assignee: SAS Institute Inc.
Inventors: James Allen Cox, Zheng Zhao

Systems and Methods for Interactive Displays Based on Associations for Machine-Guided Rule Creation

This patent is the basis for user display and interaction to choose association rules as predictors of a given outcome in a text collection (such as a topic or classification).

Patent number: 9092734

Abstract: This disclosure provides a computer-program product, system, method, and apparatus for accessing a representation of a category or item and accessing a set of multiple transactions. The transactions are processed to identify items found amongst the transactions, and the items are ordered based on an information-gain heuristic. A depth-first search for a group of best association rules is then conducted using a best-first heuristic and constraints that make the search efficient. The best rules found during the search can then be displayed to a user, along with accompanying statistics. The user can then select rules that appear to be most relevant, and further analytics can be applied to the selected rules to obtain further information about the information provided by these rules.

Type: Grant
Filed: July 21, 2014
Date of Patent: July 28, 2015
Assignee: SAS Institute Inc.
Inventors: James Allen Cox, Zheng Zhao, Barry DeVille, Arila Barnes, Jared Peterson, Samantha DuPont, Russell Albright

Fast Binary Rule Extraction for Large-Scale Text Data

This patent is the basis for extracting Boolean rules as predictors of a given outcome in a text collection (such as topic or classification). A provision is made for the removal of a rule as a noncontributor to the prediction; thus, providing rule absence (or "NOT" conditions) as a basis for the rule operation.

Patent number: 8832015

Abstract: Systems and methods for identifying data files that have a common characteristic are provided. A plurality of data files including one or more data files having a common characteristic are received. A potential rule is generated by selecting key terms from a list that satisfy a term evaluation metric, and the potential rule is evaluated using a rule evaluation metric. The potential rule is added to the rule set if the rule evaluation metric is satisfied. Based on the potential rule being added to the rule set, data files covered by the potential rule are removed from the plurality of data files. The potential rule generation and evaluation steps are repeated until a stopping criterion is met. After the stopping criterion has been met, the rule set is used to identify other data files having the common characteristic.

Type: Grant

Filed: September 21, 2012

Date of Patent: September 9, 2014

Assignee: SAS Institute Inc.

Inventors: James Allen Cox, Zheng Zhao

Normalizing Electronic Communications Using Feature Sets

This SAS patent establishes the basis for forming multiterm, sub-sentence level constructs that have unique, predictive meanings such that they operate as if they are semantic features of the sentence such as noun groups and n-grams.

Patent number: 9280747

Abstract: Electronic communications can be normalized using feature sets. For example, an electronic representation of a noncanonical communication can be received, and multiple candidate canonical versions of the noncanonical communication can be determined. A first feature set representative of the noncanonical communication can be determined by splitting the noncanonical communication into at least one n-gram and at least one k-skip-n-gram. Multiple comparison feature sets can be determined by splitting multiple terms in training data into respective comparison feature sets. Multiple Jaccard index values can be determined using the first feature set and the multiple comparison feature sets. A subset of the multiple terms in the training data in which an associated Jaccard index value exceeds a threshold can be selected. The subset of the multiple terms can be included in the multiple candidate canonical versions.

Type: Grant
Filed: October 30, 2015
Date of Patent: March 8, 2016
Assignee: SAS Institute Inc.
Inventors: Ning Jin, James Allen Cox

Social Community Identification for Automatic Document Classification

This patent provides a basis for resolving multiple potential term meanings (e.g., synonyms) based on group membership. Here, influencers determine text meaning among group members.

Patent number: 9317594

Abstract: Systems and methods for identifying data files that have a common characteristic are provided. A plurality of data files is received. The plurality of data files includes one or more data files having the common characteristic. A list of key terms is generated from the plurality of data files. Data files from the plurality of data files that have an association with a social community are identified, where the social community is defined by one or more features. The list of key terms is updated based on an analysis of the identified features. The updated list of key terms is used to identify other data files that have the common characteristic.

Type: Grant
Filed: December 27, 2012
Date of Patent: April 19, 2016
Assignee: SAS Institute Inc.
Inventors: Barry deVille, Gurpreet S. Bawa

Generating and Displaying Canonical Rule Sets with Dimensional Targets

This patent provides the basis for identifying and displaying alternative collections of predictive rules, depending on the values of controlling field values that signify alternative dimensional contexts.

Patent number: 9582761

Abstract: Systems and methods for performing analyses on data sets to display canonical rules sets with dimensional targets are disclosed. A cross-corpus rule set for a given Topic can be generated based on the entire corpus of data. A first-dimensional rule set can be generated based on a first context (e.g., based on the same Topic but using a first sub-domain of the corpus of data). A second-dimensional rule set can be generated based on a second context (e.g., based on the same Topic but using a second sub-domain of the corpus of data). Key dimensional differentiators (e.g., for each dimension, or context, of the Topic) can be determined based on a comparison of the general rule set, the first-dimensional rule set, and the second-dimensional rule set. A canonical rule set visualization can be displayed. The visualization can highlight the dimensional selectors (e.g., those tokens, or nodes, that differ between the first-dimensional rule set and the second-dimensional rule set).

Type: Grant
Filed: May 8, 2015
Date of Patent: February 28, 2017
Assignee: SAS Institute Inc.
Inventors: James Allen Cox, Barry DeVille, Zheng Zhao

Glossary

Bag of words A name for the storage approach when documents are stored as a vector representation and so the words, sequences, and contexts are lost.

Boolean operators Boolean operators are named after the mathematician and logician George Boole (1815–1864). The common Boolean operators are AND, OR, NOT. Boolean expressions consist of Boolean operators and always yield a true or false (binary) outcome and so are well-adapted to digital computing.

Boollear Boollear is a process developed by Cox and Zhao (2014) that forms predictive rules to characterize the relation between term combinations in a set of documents and a given target or category. Because the terms form linguistic rules, the process is useful for both linguistic and numerical rule-based predicative engines.

Captured response (lift) chart A measure of the accuracy of a predictive model. Given a target field that is either correctly predicted or incorrectly predicted, we measure the accuracy of the predictions by sorting the results from accurately predicted to not predicted.

Chi-squared statistic The chi-squared statistic is one of the more commonly used statistics to assess whether the categorical attributes of objects in a data collection depend on one another; for example, does eye or hair color depend on the gender attribute in a collection of data?

Collections or corpus Collections are any set of documents that are used in the text analysis.

Dimensionality reduction This is the process of expressing higher-dimensional problems and data in fewer, more easily understood dimensions.

Discriminant analysis This is a specialized form of the general problem-solving equation where a target field is expressed as a function of multiple input fields. In this case, the target is one of two classes and the inputs are specifically designed to distinguish one class from another.

Documents Documents are commonly defined as books or sections of books or essays. In text analytics, documents are also smaller parts of larger texts and may include titles, phrases, sentences, paragraphs, or even textual expressions returned in response to a search or query.

Entropy The tendency of information to degrade as it moves from sender to receiver.

Estimated precision Estimated precision is used in the Boollear process to shorten its search path and avoid generating overly specific rules. The precision is estimated by a form of additive smoothing with adjustments that favor shorter rules over longer rules.

Factor analysis This is a form of dimensionality reduction where a higher dimensional set of data is re-expressed in a lower number of dimensions that are formed into a fewer number of factors or equations.

Feature extraction This is a process of scanning input data, often text or speech, in order to derive common features that accurately reflect the data and that can then be used in various forms of mathematical expressions.

g-score Also known as likelihood-ratio or maximum likelihood statistical significance test. Used in Boollear as an information gain criterion to evaluate the correlation between predictive terms and the target in the training data set. The g-score is a form of mutual information, approximately equivalent to information gain in the binary case. Because it is distributed as chi-squared, it can also be used for statistical significance testing.

Homophily This is a general social characteristic that states that like-minded people tend to associate with one another. An associated linguistic characteristic states that words with common meanings, like communities of individuals, tend to group together in a textual expression.

Latent Dirichlet allocation LDA is a language processing technique that uses mathematical relationships to infer unobserved terms in a language model to describe observed outcomes, or topics, that are reflected in the discourse of a set of documents.

Latent semantic analysis This is an approach that uses mathematical techniques such as singular value decomposition (SCA) to discover unique and meaningful combinations of terms or expressions that succinctly describe variability among groups of terms in a collection of documents.

Latent semantic indexing Latent semantic indexing (LSI) is a text indexing and retrieval method that uses a mathematical technique called singular value decomposition (SVD) to identify patterns in the relationships between the terms and concepts contained in an unstructured collection of text.

Linear algebra Noted in the Wikipedia entry (https://en.wikipedia.org/wiki/Linear_algebra). Linear algebra is the branch of mathematics concerning linear equations and linear functions and their representations in vector spaces and associated matrix representations.

Lemmatize *See* Stem.

Matrix factorization This is an approach, drawn from linear algebra, that finds the components of a two-dimensional matrix of numbers in much the same way that we might discover that the components of the single number 6 can be expressed as 2 × 3. The discovery of simple arrays of numbers that are components of a main array that represent a collection of documents is a way of discovering the latent semantic content of the documents.

Meme A meme is a cultural artifact (named after the biological term) that captures a particular idea or behavior in a social context and is spread socially from person-to-person and group-to-group through adoption and imitation.

Mime A mime is a performer or an act of performance that communicates an idea or scene through nonverbal means, typically through imitation of the object that is being mimed or communicated.

Morpheme A morpheme is the atomic, base unit of a language and is often a word or a part of a word.

***n*-gram** An *n*-gram is an identification of adjacent term products, usually words and sometimes characters. The "*n*" signifies the number of combinations – 2, 3, 4, and so on – that are identified (two adjacent terms are called bigrams, three adjacent terms are trigrams, and so on). In the sentence "The quick brown fox jumped over the lazy dog," we have bigrams "brown-fox," "fox-jumped," "jumped-lazy," and "lazy-dog" (ignoring articles and modifiers).

Named entities Named entities are recognizable real-world objects such as persons, place names, things, organizations, and so on that are immediately recognizable and that do not require a further definition.

Noun group Nouns and modifiers are often paired together. For example, we may have a "clock" to tell the time and will recognize that an "alarm clock" is a particular kind of clock. Here, "alarm clock" is a noun group. Similarly, in addition to the noun "man" there is a specific kind of man that, for example, gives rise to the noun group "honorable man."

Ontology These are broadly used to identify high-level concepts within a range of domains and, within the concepts, identify entities, and entity relationships.

Phoneme A phoneme is a particular unit of sound that distinguishes one word from another in a particular language. While there are 26 letters in English there are over 40 unique sounds. One common phoneme, sometimes denoted by "sh," is used to distinguish sounds in ocean, sure, machine, and station, for example.

Polysemy A property of a word or term to imply the possibility of multiple meanings (from the Greek stem *poly* or *multi* and *sema* for "sign"). Words can have different meanings, depending on the context.

Predicate Predicate is a term in logic, generally meaning the part of a logical expression that is affirmed. The notion is extended to grammar to indicate the part of a sentence that describes the subject.

Principal component analysis Principal component analysis of PCA is a statistical technique to render higher dimensional data distributions into a lower dimensional, more parsimonious representation.

Roll-up terms Roll-up terms are relatively high-frequency terms that are identified during the initial document parsing and which are extracted and used as variables to characterize the documents in the collection.

Semantic field A semantic field points to an area of discourse where terms are related by meanings that are associated with the field. Subject–object relationships in a narrative that describes a vehicle driver and an automobile, for example, could form a semantic field related to automotive products and road trips.

Singular value decomposition (SVD) This is a mathematical approach to consistently create a method to summarize the term dimensionality of a set of documents and is based on linear algebra.

Sparse   The term-document matrix is almost always a sparse matrix in that most of the term-document entries are empty. There are typically many more words than documents, and usually any one document only contains a small fraction of the total number of words in the collection.

Stem (also lemmatize)   Transform various grammatical and syntactical forms of a word to a common representation; for example, "am," "are," "is" forms of the verb "to be" becomes the simplified stem form of "be."

Stop list   A list of uninformative terms that are preemptively excluded from an analysis since it is assumed they will not contribute to the analysis of inter- and intra-document meaning and behavior. Common stop words include short function words such as "the," "is," "at," "which," and "on."

Taxonomy   This is a general term for an elaboration of various classes of objects. The childhood guessing game of "animal," "mineral," "vegetable," establishes a taxonomy of these three high-level categories. Taxonomies are useful in text analytics since identified members of a taxonomy can then take on attributes of the whole taxonomy.

Support vector machine (SVM)   This is a linear model that is used to characterize and predict instances in data in one of two categories. The technique computes a linear hyperplane that optimally separates the two classes. Marginal instances that are close to the categories that are being distinguishes form a support vector.

Tenfold cross validation   Cross validation is an effective way to use validation data to cross check sample-based data models. Here, the training data is randomly partitioned into 10 equal size subsamples that are then reused as validation data sets.

Term-document matrix   This is a typical way of storing the collection of documents as an internal computer representation that can be manipulated analytically to yield text analytic products.

Varimax   A method of rotating dimensions in factor analysis, first proposed by Henry Kaiser in 1958, and employed in IQ tests, for example, where it is used to rotate the axes of the dimensions to line up as closely as possible with the individual test questions.

Words or terms   A term is often what we usually consider as a word; terms may also refer to punctuation, phrases – including noun phrases – and other multiword terms.

Worth statistic A worth statistic is sometimes used to translate a statistical test of independence such as a chi-squared statistic into a strength of relationship expressed as a probability between 0 and 1.

z-score Also called a standard score. This is a score based on the normal distribution. Typically, a score may be 1, 2, or 3 standard deviations above or below the average, or mean, of a standard distribution. This facilitates comparing numbers according to a common – "standard" – scale.

Index

Page numbers followed by *f* and *t* refer to figures and tables, respectively.